The
ANIMAL
COMMUNICATOR'S
GUIDE
Through Life, Loss and Love

133.9

The
ANIMAL
COMMUNICATOR'S
GUIDE
Through Life, Loss and Love

Pea Horsley

HAY HOUSE

Carlsbad, California • New York City • London • Sydney
Johannesburg • Vancouver • Hong Kong • New Delhi

First published and distributed in the United Kingdom by:
Hay House UK Ltd, Astley House, 33 Notting Hill Gate, London W11 3JQ
Tel: +44 (0)20 3675 2450; Fax: +44 (0)20 3675 2451
www.hayhouse.co.uk

Published and distributed in the United States of America by:
Hay House Inc., PO Box 5100, Carlsbad, CA 92018-5100
Tel: (1) 760 431 7695 or (800) 654 5126
Fax: (1) 760 431 6948 or (800) 650 5115
www.hayhouse.com

Published and distributed in Australia by:
Hay House Australia Ltd, 18/36 Ralph St, Alexandria NSW 2015
Tel: (61) 2 9669 4299; Fax: (61) 2 9669 4144
www.hayhouse.com.au

Published and distributed in the Republic of South Africa by:
Hay House SA (Pty) Ltd, PO Box 990, Witkoppen 2068
Tel/Fax: (27) 11 467 8904
www.hayhouse.co.za

Published and distributed in India by:
Hay House Publishers India, Muskaan Complex, Plot No.3, B-2,
Vasant Kunj, New Delhi 110 070
Tel: (91) 11 4176 1620; Fax: (91) 11 4176 1630
www.hayhouse.co.in

Distributed in Canada by:
Raincoast Books, 2440 Viking Way, Richmond, B.C. V6V 1N2
Tel: (1) 604 448 7100; *Fax:* (1) 604 270 7161; www.raincoast.com

Text © Pea Horsley, 2014

A catalogue record for this book is available from the British Library.

ISBN: 978-1-78180-334-9

Printed and bound in Great Britain by TJ International Ltd, Padstow, Cornwall

This book is dedicated to...
All those facing loss, grieving for a loved
one or caring for the grieving.
All the animals in heaven and on Earth who
are a constant source of inspiration.
And Morgan – who gave me my wings.

Contents

Foreword

I have lost count of the number of people who have said to me 'I'd love to have been a vet, but I couldn't cope with putting pets to sleep.' And, as every vet will freely acknowledge, euthanasia is the most difficult and distressing task to have to carry out, especially as it happens on a regular basis. There are few careers that involve the frequent and intentional taking of life.

But for most vets, the greatest difficulty does not arise from actually carrying out the euthanasia. In fact, as long as a pet's life is ended to prevent pain and suffering, and is ended calmly and peacefully, there can be a certain sense of satisfaction in bringing that life to a close. The main problem for the majority of vets is coping with the distress of the person or family who has been caring for that pet, often for many years.

Vets have little training in helping clients through the shock and grief of losing a pet. In particular there seem to be no simple answers to the torrent of questions that flow both before and after euthanasia.

◇ 'How can I be sure it's the right time to let him go?'

◇ 'How can I let her know I'm doing this for her?'

◇ 'Will she understand what's going on?'

◇ 'Do animals have a soul? Do they go to heaven?'

◇ 'How can I let him know I loved him?'

◇ 'I feel she is still around – I can feel her presence. How can this be?'

Every vet who has been through such questioning and puzzled over how to give a useful answer, and everybody who has ever had to say goodbye to a loved pet, or has to go through that experience in the future, should read *The Animal Communicator's Guide Through Life, Loss and Love* from cover to cover.

Pea Horsley is able to give realistic and comforting answers to all these questions and more, both from her moving account of losing Morgan, her beagle, and from the many pets she has met and communicated with, both before and after their deaths.

Death seems to be the last taboo in British society, and grieving for a lost pet particularly so. Many of my own clients have said they felt embarrassed to display any signs of grief to friends or work colleagues. Pea explains the process of grief, how normal it is to feel the loss of a pet and how to help to resolve the emotions of bereavement.

The Animal Communicator's Guide Through Life, Loss and Love is a book dealing with a sad and potentially depressing subject, but anyone who reads it will find it comforting, practical and – remarkably – positive and uplifting.

Richard Allport
BVetMed, VetMFHom, MRCVS
Author of *Natural Healthcare for Pets, Heal Your Dog the Natural Way* and *Heal Your Cat the Natural Way*

Acknowledgements

◇

It has taken a couple of years for this book to emerge. Time was needed to allow the blessings that follow loss to flourish fully. This is a book that couldn't be rushed, hurried, cajoled or demanded into existence; it just needed to flow in its own good time as and when it was ready. I have been supported during the writing of it by the guidance of many loving, helpful, generous and talented people and animals, and I wish to thank them with all my heart.

I am very grateful to Michelle Pilley, Amy Kiberd and Louise Hay for taking this book into their hands and hearts, as well as the rest of the Hay House Publishers UK team for their inclusive, sensitive and professional expertise.

Purrs go to my copy editor, Lizzie Hutchins, for her feline focus, direct honesty and sensitive understanding of animal communication. Recognition also to the four-pawed felines behind her work: Wimpole, Tinker, and Bonetti on his lofty throne in heaven.

To all of Morgan's veterinary team: Mr Phakkey (allopathic), Mr Greenway (acupuncture) and, as Morgan put it, 'my favourite vet', Mr Richard Allport (homoeopathic/holistic). A special thank you to you, Richard, for being so supportive of animal communication and writing the foreword to this book at a time when much of the veterinary world is still challenging the credibility and effectiveness of this much-needed work.

Thank you to Bliss for permission to reproduce the lyrics of 'Keep the Faith' from the album *Flying Free* (Blissfulmusic, 1997), and to Hay House, Inc., Carlsbad, CA, for permission to quote from *Archangel Michael Oracle Cards* © Doreen Virtue, 2009.

Thank you to Lynne Lazenby for advising me and being there for Morgan, and to Jo Sayers and Roger Simonsz for reading some of the early drafts. Thank you also to Erica Town for helping me with the final proofs.

Thanks also to Caroline Mylon, Amanda Henry-May and Jonathan Warhurst and Mike Davies. Not forgetting my adopted Mother, Mary, for endless love and support.

Thank you to Linda Tucker for your generous Introduction to this book and for your inspirational conservation work leading the Global White Lion Protection Trust.

Jane Hargreaves, thank you for caring for Morgan while I was teaching and for all of the much-appreciated behind-the-scenes support over the years.

Belinda Wright and Laura Scott, thank you for sharing your spiritual home when a safe haven was needed just after Morgan transitioned and when I was completing this book.

Thanks to: Lynn Smith and Sandra Houston, for coming over to care for Morgan when he was struggling and neither Jo nor I could be at home, and dear Saffie, for being his friend, the long walks and trips to the pub.

Mark O'Brien and Sue Henderson, for often having Morgan to stay in your home along with your own beloved dog and for being such a loving friend to him. And thank you, Roxy, for sharing your bed so graciously.

Jenny Scott and Tony Simpson, for such fantastic support during the challenging times of Morgan's stroke and seizure and during the big photo shoot, and for being a great friend to Morgan.

Sandra Dalmejer, for your endless encouragement over the years and more recently whenever I wobbled and said, 'I just don't know if I can do this.' For caring for Morgan when he was younger and healthy and then older and frail. And love to Buddy, now back home in heaven.

Johanna Town, for being encouraging throughout the process of writing this book, and not forgetting devil's advocate – your favourite role. Thank you for persuading me to bring a dog into our lives. Little did we know the huge impact Morgan would have on our future.

Thank you to all the guardians who have generously shared their joy, their loss, their pain and their love so publicly to benefit all who read their stories. You are courageous and caring people and your stories are examples of the best of humanity.

And to all the animals, without whom this book would not exist, thank you for helping me craft your stories. You continue to inspire and amaze me with your great depths of generosity, your passion for life and your enormous never-faltering love. Your understanding of the connectedness of consciousness and truth of existence is very humbling.

Finally, thank you to my guides, who offer protection, strength and encouragement at all the right times and who help me stay on my path, including my darling Texas, my black beauty Bodhi and the light of my life – Morgan.

Introduction

❦

'We are all connected, all of the time, across any distance'
– this is the key to animal communication as evidenced
in Pea Horsley's beautifully written autobiography, although the
message does not come directly from her, but from Morgan, her
first dog and interspecies educator.

The insights you will gain from this book are more
profound than anything you could ever imagine, and yet so
simple and so obvious. Without doubt, animal communication
will change your life; and if you have all but lost hope in
humanity, given the devastation our species has wreaked on
this magnificent Earth, it will offer you the most effective
way to restore your original contract with nature – and help
save our Earth.

When you live in wild pride-lands, together with the apex
predator and the other natural kingdoms in the food chain and
great cycle of life, as I do, you realize that God is very much alive,
and so, too, the Force of Love that unites all of divine creation.

We are, indeed, all connected. I am fortunate enough to cohabit with the last White Lions in their endemic wilderness lands, and all the other interconnected creatures of their natural ecosystem. Every day, I wake to the birdsong, and every night I go to sleep with the roar of the king of animals on the distant horizons, and I witness the soul-bond of unconditional love and respect that exists in natural biodiversity between all creatures, great and small, wise and wonderful – even, unlikely as it may seem, between predator and prey.

We all lived this way once, as the magnificent paintings in the caves of Lascaux and other prehistoric sites remind us, not in fear but in love and reverence for all of creation – an idyllic condition we all know deep in our heart of hearts, and which we yearn to restore more than anything. Even if you live in the city, as I did when I worked in the fashion centres of Europe, uprooted from nature, alienated and separated, you still know in your soul essence that there is a state of grace, but it can only be reached by helping to restore Paradise on Earth, the gift that the great Creative Force – in whatever name you choose to name It – lovingly gave over into humanity's care.

Today, in the midst of a global meltdown in all matters man-made, not only our impact on climate, animal communication is the most powerful tool we humans possess to re-establish a loving and meaningful relationship with the real world. Through simple, straightforward language and astounding real-life examples, Pea Horsley's book will help you find the way back to a meaningful existence with yourself and the other magnificent animals who share this planet.

The facts speak for themselves. Animal communication is a natural attribute we all once possessed. Although this ability dates back to the most ancient of times, it is critically relevant to the modern day, and *the key* not only to protecting our planet but also to saving ourselves.

Linda Tucker
CEO, Global White Lion Protection Trust
Shamanic title: Keeper of the White Lions
Author of *Mystery of the White Lions* and *Saving the White Lions*

Author's Note

The Animal Communicator's Guide Through Life, Loss and Love is much more than a collection of communications gathered over time – this book contains my heart and soul and those of my clients as we bring you our personal journeys.

The chapters follow a chronological order which allows you to progress along a path led by your guides – the animals.

The reason for this book has always been, since my dear teacher, Morgan, planted the seed, to offer a source of comfort, support and deeper understanding to those who are grieving the loss of a beloved animal companion.

If you are grieving at this time, please accept my deepest sympathy. I can understand the depth of the pain you are feeling as you come to terms with losing a beloved animal. As you read through the pages of this book you will come to understand that you are not alone with these feelings. Many people have shared a sacred relationship with these incredible beings who truly understand what you are going through. It is my most sincere hope that this book will bring you comfort and support through this most difficult time.

Please Note

Animal communication, however valuable, is not a substitute for the expert diagnosis of a trusted veterinarian. If you feel your animal is unwell, please seek out a reputable medical professional who is caring, compassionate and respectful to you and your animal.

Chapter 1

'We Are All Connected'

∼◈∼

'We are all connected, all of the time,
across any distance.'
MORGAN

This is the one story I never wanted to write. It is a true story and it is about my own dog, Morgan.

Behind me lies a huge soul in a fragile body. He's part beagle, part Jack Russell and maybe there's even a bit of Labrador thrown in there for fun. His eyes are soulful dark chocolate and his lips thick black, which sometimes makes him appear a little like a smiling clown. But not today. Today he's struggling. Today he finds it hard to walk. He's not really interested in water. In fact he's stopped drinking it altogether except when I add it to some cooked coley to create the morning delicacy of fishy soup, a dish he has always loved.

Today is a heartbreaking day, because today he is sad. I feel it deeply. My tears fight to get to the surface and I battle unsuccessfully to keep them down. I know his life force is slipping away. He is slipping away, to a better place for his soul. I know this, but it still hurts. His body is worn out now and frustrating him most of the time. I can see that. I can feel it. I connect with it every day and I feel tired too. It's hard to be there for my clients, listening to their anxieties and agonies about their elderly or dying animals, especially when they are dogs. I'm professional and hide my feelings, but sometimes when I put the phone down I cry as their pain strikes a chord with my own.

I glance over my right shoulder to where Morgan is lying in his tartan-patterned bed by the garden doors and he tells me to keep going, to continue writing this for others to read as a source of comfort. This dear dog, Morgan, has instructed me to write a book about what it is to live, to let go, to die... and how life continues when the physical body ceases to exist.

Morgan is my biggest love to date. Yes, a dog. But not 'just a dog'.

Not 'Just a Dog'

Morgan is the one who introduced me to animal communication and changed my life forever.

When my pale ginger cat Winston passed over I thought my heart would never be broken in the same way again. Winston was my teenage love-affair and I adored him. If I had to compare, though, I'd say my love for Morgan is on another level. I'm older now and this love is about being in service to others, not about a cat comforting a teenager through offering unconditional love and acceptance. We've moved on from there.

I first laid eyes on Morgan when he was lying on his left side upon a thick duvet in the Mayhew Animal Home administration office. He was at full luxurious stretch. I bent down to stroke his beagle-like head and he looked up at me with soft, gentle chocolate-coloured eyes and I felt safe. Up to this point I had been wary of dogs after being bitten and chased off a farm by Jack Russell terriers and lunged at by a teeth-baring Labrador.

At the time Morgan was probably about seven or eight years old and the rescue home felt he wouldn't cope well in a kennel environment so he was being fostered by a member of staff who took him to the office during the day and allowed him to lie on her sofa at home in the evening. But he wasn't frail in any shape or form – in fact he had a vibrancy about him. He was lying there totally relaxed, with sparkling eyes and a cheeky smile. He looked great but, as I was to discover, he wasn't perfect by any means.

After passing the home check, I was able to adopt Morgan and he moved in. All rescued animals need time to settle, but after a number of weeks I felt Morgan was feeling sad and I believed I must be doing something wrong. I was a big cat-lover, having grown up with them, but I didn't know dogs.

By chance the Mayhew e-mailed me about an animal communication workshop they were hosting. I thought this was a subtle way of saying 'learn to read your dog's body language', so I went along, hoping I would be able to understand Morgan a little more. I was astounded to hear the teacher say it was possible to talk to animals.

With a theatre background and a very successful 15-year career as a stage manager, I considered myself grounded, and I was sceptical too. Yet at this workshop I discovered I could communicate with a rabbit through his photo and that my partner, who was at the time a complete stranger to me, could communicate with my cat, Texas, through the photo I'd brought along of him. It was weird because it was as though she'd had a private viewing of my home: she was able to describe the colour of my sofa, Texas's favourite spot in the garden and what he loved to sit on. That first workshop challenged my belief system, which was based on the premise that animals couldn't communicate. I wanted to know more, so I attended another one.

On the second workshop I had my 'lightbulb' moment: the sudden revelation that I was meant to be an animal communicator and that everything I had experienced up to this point had been preparation for what was to come.

Many years later I was having an e-mail conversation with a vet and columnist for a well-known broadsheet when he commented: 'I can see that your calling is to do exactly what you are doing. You are opening a door to a different way of seeing consciousness in sentient beings.'

At further training workshops I found myself connecting with animals who had passed over, which actually felt like the most natural thing in the world. It was surprising that a self-confessed atheist could do this and I really had to address what I thought was my truth, as my beliefs didn't bear any relation to my current experiences.

When I felt confident enough at communicating with animals, I sat down with Morgan to understand why he was sad. I found myself picturing his previous guardians in my mind. They were an elderly couple. The man had a walking stick. I felt the woman had passed over and he had been taken into care. Morgan had been taken to death row, where his life would have ended if the animal rescue hadn't stepped in, an act for which I will be forever grateful.

It may be hard to understand at this point that I was able to help Morgan by communicating both with him and his deceased guardian. It helps to experience animal communication directly to really grasp that it is possible. But throughout this book I will give you evidence of my telepathic communications with other people's animal companions which have been verified by the guardian themself or proven to be correct by the animal's own vet.

After my communication with Morgan, the change in him was instant. He was able to move on from his past and settle in with his new family, and because he was able to do this, Texas, who up to this time had shunned him, welcomed him too – up to a point. After all, it was his home first and he was *the boss*.

Morgan wasn't the only one who was transformed. I gave up my career as a stage manager and founded Animal Thoughts, an animal communication service. Business grew through word of mouth and I started to teach workshops across the world to people interested in connecting with their own animals. I found myself regularly communicating with animals facing the end of their physical life as well as those who had already transitioned to the afterlife. Communicating with an animal whose soul has returned home is one of the greatest privileges of my work.

What is Animal Communication?

You may have never heard of animal communication before and could be wondering how it works.

Animal communication is an intuitive exchange of non-verbal information between humans and animals. 'Inter-species communication' or 'animal telepathy' refer to the same method of connection. But don't confuse this with the terms 'horse whisperer' or 'dog listener', which are forms of reading an animal's body language and understanding a particular species psychology.

In animal communication information is sent and received non-verbally by intention using the senses. The details – thoughts, feelings, sensations – are electromagnetic energy. So, animal communication is essentially an exchange of energetic information.

This means, for example, that a human doesn't have to talk tortoise and a tortoise doesn't have to talk human for them to understand each other. I am using the word 'talk' in the loosest sense to encompass non-verbal energetic exchange of information. The communication is subtle, sensitive and takes dedication and practice to fine-tune. To be skilled, you have to work at it, just as you would when learning an instrument, sport or language. But it can be done.

This is just a brief outline, because this isn't a 'how to' book, but you will find out more about the whiskers and tails of animal communication as you read on, and you can use this in attempting to connect with your own animals.

For now, I would like to introduce some interesting truths about animals in relation to emotion, intelligence and consciousness. These concepts will give you the foundation for what you are about to read.

Our Place in the World

Humans often believe they are above the animal kingdom. The truth is they are a *part* of the animal kingdom – humans are animals too.

It is now more commonly accepted that non-human animals have emotional traits and powers of communication beyond verbal expression. You may have heard of Bella, the dog who mourned the loss of her best friend, a beaver, in a display of emotion that clearly showed she felt loss. When Beavis the beaver was alive, he and Bella were inseparable friends. They lived and loved together, and when Beavis died, Bella lay by his side whimpering for hours. Dogs nearby played with balls and wagged their tails without a care in the world, but Bella lay inconsolable next to her best friend, sometimes putting her head on his back, sometimes licking him or nuzzling into his large beaver body.

You may have also seen coverage of the friendship between another Bella, this time a stray dog, and Tarra, an elephant at the Tennessee Elephant Sanctuary. They played and ate together and often slept together in a barn. When Bella suffered a severe spinal cord injury, she had to be separated from Tarra while undergoing treatment. Tarra stood vigil for three weeks beside a gate to the sanctuary office, although she had 2,200 acres to roam in. Their reunion was breathtaking: they were obviously feeling joy at seeing one another. When Bella was attacked a year later, possibly by coyotes, the sanctuary believed Tarra found her body and carried it to a spot where they had often spent time together. 'The idea that she couldn't leave that body and brought it back home is just heartbreaking, but so inspiring,' said Robert Atkinson, CEO of The Elephant Sanctuary.

Scientists now accept that animals are intelligent. In new research published in the *Proceedings of the National Academy of Science*, scientists at the Indian Institute of Science have found that bottlenose dolphins are able to call each other by a specific name. Just like humans who respond to a verbal name, dolphins are able to identify copies of their own unique signature whistles. This level of communication is beyond general signalling to find food or warn about danger and much more advanced than many scientists previously believed.

We are aware that animals are able to make decisions about what they play with, what they eat, where they sleep and who they have as friends. So wouldn't it also make sense that they are able to make decisions about a whole heap of other things too? Take their health, for instance.

Some animals self-medicate by choosing plants that occur naturally in the wild and provide the essential oils, algae, clay and other natural remedies that they need. This process is known as zoopharmacognosy (from the Greek *zoo*, meaning 'animal', *pharma*, meaning 'drug' and *gnosy* meaning 'knowing'), which was a phrase given by Dr Eloy Rodriguez, a biochemist at Cornell University. His laboratory was instrumental in the study of self-medicating animals in the wild.

If animals are able to make decisions about plants to improve their health, surely this is an indication that they are aware of when their physical body is sick? Could they also be aware when their body is dying? Are they capable of knowing how much time they have left in their physical form? These are interesting questions to consider.

The Oxford English Dictionary defines consciousness as 'the state of being conscious, the fact of awareness by the mind of itself and the world, one's awareness or perception of something'. Do animals have conscious awareness?

On 7 December 2012 a group of prominent scientists met at the University of Cambridge at the first annual Francis Crick Memorial Conference on Consciousness in Human and Non-Human Animals. The group consisted of cognitive scientists, neuropharmacologists, neurophysiologists, neuroanatomists and computational neuroscientists. In the presence of Professor Stephen Hawking, the conference participants signed the Cambridge Declaration of Consciousness, in which they publicly made the declaration that: 'The weight of evidence indicates that humans are not unique in possessing the neurological substrates that generate consciousness.'

The eminent scientists made a list of the non-human animals that they considered to have consciousness. This included all mammals, birds and many other creatures, including the octopus.

Former executive director of the Mind Science Foundation Joseph Dial said to camera that night:

'This was a very historic evening. What I observed happening tonight... [was] that people finally came to the realization that the way in which we... understood animal consciousness was very primitive and very backward, and everyone tonight said what they've always thought... that animal consciousness and human consciousness are of

such similarity that we have to ask ourselves how we treat
animals and why we treat them the way that we do.'

Three eminent neuroscientists publicly concluded that 'Non-human animals have the neuroanatomical, neurochemical, and neurophysiological substrates of conscious states, along with the capacity to exhibit intentional behaviours.'

So, scientists agree that the dog next to you or the cat on your lap or the horse in your paddock and all the other creatures in your life are not insensate machines – they are glorious, bright and aware sentient beings who experience consciousness.

Why this need for a scientific declaration of animal emotion, intelligence and consciousness? As a society we have been taught not to trust our gut feelings until we are informed by a science-based source that they are correct. Setting aside whether that approach is itself correct, perhaps this declaration will help improve our treatment of animals.

Moving into New Awareness

You're about to read a book in which animals telepathically communicate their life and health needs and explain how they view dying and what they feel about death. Some communications are from animals whose soul has already left its physical form.

My journey with Morgan will continue through the book and you will learn about his health challenges, courage and love as we approach his death and how he continues to connect with me now that he has transitioned into non-physical form.

Discovering that the soul essence continues after the body has died has had a huge impact on me, and I now find myself able to talk about death without feeling scared or terribly upset. I am also able to help others. By the end of this book I hope you will come to accept what Morgan told me early on in our relationship: 'We are all connected, all of the time, across any distance.'

It took me a while to truly believe this, but the communications I have had with animals who have crossed over have been the proof I needed to silence my sceptical mind.

You may be facing having to let go of your own animal's physical presence in your life. You may have this book in your hands right now because you are grieving for an animal who has already passed over. You may be reading it because you are caring for an animal who is elderly or gradually declining in health. Maybe you are simply curious to know animals' views on life after death.

Whatever brings you here, I hope that you find this book uplifting for your mind, comforting for your heart and enlightening for your soul. You are holding the book Morgan wanted to share with you. It was written for you, with our love.

To ease you into the world of animal communication, let me first share a story about a cat called Willow and her guardian, Jane.

Part I

RESPECTING FREE WILL

*'Although other animals may
be different from us, this does not
make them less than us.'*
MARC BEKOFF

Chapter 2
Willow, the Sophia Loren of the Cat World

༄

'Stop trying to please everyone else and put yourself first.
They will show you more love and respect if you do.'
WILLOW

Jane approached me back in May 2007. She was 40 years old, the director of her own marketing company and an experienced guardian to cats, having lived with them all her life. She wanted me to communicate with her 15-year-old cat, Willow, but to understand why she made contact about Willow, we first need to hear about my communication with her rabbit.

Jane had found me the year before through a search for alternative animal healing when her rabbit, Peter, had problems with overgrown teeth and was in danger of being put to sleep.

To connect with Peter I looked at his photograph and went through my process to forge a link. I began by inhaling and exhaling slowly, using my breathing to relax my body and mind. Then I moved my focus into my heart and imagined reaching out from my heart to Peter's heart, sending him the frequency of my loving intention. I spoke to him silently in my mind, explaining who I was and why I was linking in with him. We began to communicate and I received his thought forms in my mind, hearing them as my own inner voice. He told me there was still a spike on one of his teeth and it had caused another ulcer. He also told me it was not his time to pass over.

Despite her vet having already given Peter a dental inspection and treatment, Jane chose to act on his information and made another appointment. The vet discovered Peter was right and a spike had been missed. The information Peter had communicated saved his life and he went on to live for over two more years. As the communication was life-changing, literally, Jane decided she needed to hear from all her other animals and Willow, her favourite cat, would have to be first.

Being based in Gloucestershire, she opted for another distant communication. I can go to people's homes to visit their animals, but due to geographical location the majority of guardians opt for distant communication.

Jane e-mailed me a photo of Willow and the questions she wanted me to put to her. This time she wasn't looking for a specific answer to a physical illness; what she really wanted to know was what was going on in Willow's mind and whether she was happy.

> *'She has been my cat since she was eight weeks old and she is 16 years old next month. The bond between the two of us seems immense. She talks to me, says "Hello" in a cat meow and I am just captivated by her. This one will certainly break me when it's time for goodbye. Could you just have a general chat, as I am fascinated by the connection I have with her? I love all my animals, but the connection with Willow seems so strong.'*

When I looked at Willow's picture I saw a cat exuding elegance. Her fur was a subtle tabby blend of toffee, coffee and chocolate and she was lying on a fawn-coloured cushion on a sofa, her face towards the camera. Her right leg was draped beautifully over the left, revealing two pristine white paws. She boasted a white heart-shaped chest and her whiskers, too, were milky white, proud and wide. Her pale pistachio eyes immediately commanded respect. Willow was posing for the camera and waiting.

Many animals seem to expect me when I communicate with them, but it doesn't matter if they are busy doing something or even sleeping, because the connection is energetic. It goes beyond the external behaviour to discover what the animal is feeling on a deeper level. It transcends body language. It also transcends space. I don't need to have the animal in front of me – a good photo is enough for me to build a link with them, whether they are still in physical form or have passed over.

The moment I connected with Willow I heard a loud *roarrrr* inside my head. Was Willow roaring at me? This was the first time a cat had done that during a communication. She certainly had a huge energy, which was very strong and spirited. When I felt her looking back at me it was as if she was looking straight through me. She was confident, in charge and not a cat to be messed with, despite her beguiling air of sophistication.

The next thing I heard inside my mind was: 'The queen.' These were unusual impressions from an animal, but I wrote them down anyway, because although they meant nothing to me, they might mean something to Willow's guardian.

I continued to sense as much as I could about Willow while holding her in awe. Once I'd received a number of details I e-mailed Jane some first impressions, which I asked her to verify so we could both check the connection.

Impressions of Willow

'Jane, I feel that Willow is a lion in a cat's body. The first thing I received was her giving me one of her best roars.'

'This made me laugh,' wrote Jane. 'She has always sat in the position of the Sphinx, but with her front paws elegantly crossed in front of her. Does she really think she's a lion? I do tell her she's a *sphinx*. Do you think I've brainwashed her?'

On the contrary, I thought, *Willow is doing the brainwashing.*

Jane confirmed my feeling that Willow had a big presence and was very strong-minded: 'It's either Willow's way or no way.'

'Willow says she likes to sleep up by your chest and heart area,' I went on, 'but you prefer her to sleep lower down the bed by your feet.'

'Oh yes, Willow is a well-cosseted cat. My husband is pushed to the very edge, I am in the middle and Willow spreads out on the other side. However much I try and move her lower down the bed she won't have any of it and walks all over me to get back up by my pillow and sometimes even on my head!'

My next impression was a little more private: 'Willow tells me that you share special moments in the bathroom with her.'

'Mmmm, I wouldn't say "special moments",' Jane replied, 'but my bathroom is my sanctuary. There I am no longer a director, a wife, a mother, a sister... I am just me, lying in bubbles for a few minutes with nobody asking me anything. But Willow will often time it that as soon as I climb into the bath she cries at the door to be let in. I'll clamber out, dripping wet, and open the door, and she'll have a drink of water from her bowl, which she insists on having in the bathroom, and then lie on the bath mat waiting for me. If I decide to stay in the bath for longer than usual, she will get bored and ask to be let out. The whole clambering-out routine will happen all over again.'

So, those were what Willow considered *special moments*.

I went onto the next impression Willow wished to share with Jane: 'I adore her.'

Later Jane told me, 'Now that is what I wanted to hear... the purrs and cuddles and rubbing were enough to let me know she loved me, but for her to communicate that was such a special moment.'

These details were just the beginning of a larger tapestry which was about to be unveiled.

The next impression I sent Jane was: 'You have two daughters who are lots of fun, smiley and happy.'

'No,' Jane's heart dropped. 'I don't have any daughters, just one son.'

I felt so sure Willow was talking about two daughters I decided to bring it up again later when we were on the phone.

We continued with further impressions and Jane was happy that I had made a connection with Willow. We arranged a telephone appointment.

The Queen's Speech

I began by explaining the procedure and that Jane could interrupt me at any point to ask questions, take notes or seek clarification. When she was ready, we began.

Rather than simply answering Jane's questions, Willow wanted to say one or two things of her own. One of the first was: 'I am the queen.'

'I've always called her that!' Jane exclaimed. 'I can't believe that now she's telling you in no uncertain terms that she *is* the queen. I also sing her a little song.'

'How does it go?' I asked.

Jane started to sing it:

> *'Willow is the queen of the May and the June,*
> *Willow is the queen of the sun and the moon,*
> *Willow is the queen of the land and the sea,*
> *Willow is the queen who belongs to me!'*

I loved the fact that Jane sang to Willow. Continuing, I said, 'As well as referring to herself as a queen, or rather *the* queen, I feel she has a very Sophia Loren quality to her. She's got a strong feminine strength and is really quite beautiful. In fact, Willow *is* the Sophia Loren of the cat world.'

Jane looked across at Willow, who was yet again lying Sphinx-like across her cushion with her front legs crossed. She said, 'Willow has just blinked at me very slowly as if to say "I am."'

This made me laugh. It was very Willow. She had good self-esteem and considered herself stunning. If only all females had such a healthy view of themselves.

Jane was happy with the communication so far and it was now time to bring the two daughters up again. I knew I needed to be as delicate as possible because of what I was about to say.

'May I ask, have you ever lost any children, Jane?'

'Yes, I had two miscarriages before having my son.'

'Do you happen to know if they were girls?'

'No, the doctors never told me. One was at 10 weeks and the other at 15 weeks.'

'Would the timing make sense if I said one of the girls would be 11 now and the other 12?'

There was a prolonged silence and then in a quiet voice Jane answered, 'Yes.'

'Willow is giving me the name "Bethany",' I said. 'Does that make sense to you?'

'Oh my God! Nobody, but *nobody*, knew that was the name I had chosen for the second pregnancy: *Bethany*. Bethany Jane. Nobody would know that – you certainly wouldn't – but Willow does!'

Jane felt herself go cold with shock.

'Did she say anything else?'

'Yes. She said, "She has two daughters. They are lots of fun – smiley, happy girls. I like the little one, Bethany, the best."'

Jane went quiet and I felt she was going to cry, but then I heard Willow say, 'Tell her Bethany is the naughty one.'

I repeated it for Jane, who burst out laughing. 'It's typical of Willow to make me laugh if I feel down, and only she could make a judgement about someone being naughty, someone I have never met.'

'She's going on to talk about your son.'

'What does she say?'

'He has a lot to learn.'

Jane laughed. After the call she passed Willow's message on to her 11-year-old son, Jake, who was surprised and asked, 'What does she mean?'

Jane helped me understand. 'I know exactly what Willow means. Willow wraps humans – well, *me* – around her little finger. She will cry and I am there, but not Jake. She will often get a lump in her blanket which simply needs straightening – a queen *cannot* lie on a creased blanket – and she'll walk in a circle moaning. Jake will tell her to shush, but not me – I'll be there straightening it out.'

Willow also had her own views on Jane's husband: 'Willow says, "Derek is nice, but he doesn't appreciate Jane enough. She works very hard and is very generous. He needs to share the jobs more."'

She even expressed her thoughts about the rabbit.

'I feel Willow is a bit jealous of your rabbit,' I told Jane.

'Yes, she licks her lips and starts hissing if Peter comes up,' she confirmed.

'Willow sees you all as equal. She's as much a member of the family as anyone else. I sense that she's a bit stiff in her shoulders and a bit more cantankerous than usual, more demanding, but she says, "There's nothing to worry about. I eat well, sleep well and feel very strong."'

Jane laughed again.

I finished the communication by giving her Willow's final message: '*Love, love, love.*'

'You have summed her up so well,' Jane said. 'I knew she was a character but now I have evidence, which I feel I can trust because of all the details you couldn't possibly have known, including the name "Bethany" – and all this from her photo!'

Later she wrote:

'Both my son and husband were surprised by how much Willow communicated and for days afterwards they both seemed to be on their best behaviour whenever she came into the room. It was almost "Better behave or Willow will tell Pea." I must admit that for a few days after the communication Jake was up like a shot if Willow moaned, but that didn't last long.

The communication was simply fabulous. It filled me with such happiness to have evidence that Willow did know what was going on in our lives. I wasn't frightened or nervous and it was delivered in such a caring way. It was so appropriate.'

I was impressed by Willow myself. She had tuned in to Jane's energy and understood that she had lost not one but two of her children. As well as this, she had been aware of their characters in their soul existence. In the most extraordinary way she had been able to heal Jane's aching heart.

Willow's Health Deteriorates

On 9 December 2009 Jane asked me to communicate with Willow again. 'Tests have revealed her kidneys are deteriorating rapidly,' she told me. 'I feel devastated. She's 18, but I'm not ready to let her go. I'd like one more year, please. Can you find out if there's anything I can do?'

I connected with Willow by looking at her photo and once more began to take notes of the impressions she was giving me:

'Nothing is too much of a problem. Willow sometimes needs a hand up onto the sofa, but she doesn't mind.

Her sense of dignity is strong.

She adores biscuits (for humans) – "A lady should be able to eat whatever she likes."

Lower spine/coccyx – arthritic feeling. Hips and back legs are worse – the sensation is grating.

She is very calm and serene.

"I am not struggling so badly, dear one. Don't worry yet. Just keep calm."

She loves it when Jane admires her white paws and white chest.'

When Jane and I started our phone call she asked me not to tell her if I felt Willow would transition soon. She asked her first question: 'I really want to know what else she wants me to do for her.'

'Just keep calm,' Willow replied. 'You are doing everything perfectly. Don't worry any more.'

'That cat knows me far too well – I worry when I've nothing to worry about,' Jane said.

'I like the warmth,' Willow continued, 'a heated pad, a source of warmth. You know this.'

'I was about to buy a heat pad for her,' Jane said, surprised. 'It's been on my mind for a while. Another thing I need to know is, am I doing anything wrong?'

'Not a thing, dear,' Willow replied.

'I just want to understand a bit more what's going on,' Jane told me. 'I still feel Willow has a huge energy about her, but I do wonder sometimes if I'm just *hoping* she has.'

I explained, 'Her energy is waning, but she is still happy with life. She still feels as strong mentally as she's always been and she's positive, upbeat, calm, sophisticated and unflustered.'

'I know she's an old cat and is slower,' Jane said, 'but she's probably the most spoiled and loved cat that ever purred on this planet. This one is my little soul mate. I want to make sure that she is happy and not in too much pain.'

Willow replied, 'My lower back and legs ache quite consistently, but I am peaceful.'

'What does she want me to do?'

'Everything you're doing now,' said Willow. 'Just love me.'

Much later, looking back at the communication, Jane realized that Willow was protecting her from the full extent of her situation and at the same time preparing her for the inevitable. She reflected:

'Like a mother protects a child, Willow was protecting me. I am sure she knew that I would have had the most miserable Christmas knowing that this was the last one with my girl, and she chose to spare my feelings. I hoped in my heart that you were going to say, "Oh, Willow is fine, she has such huge energy and she's going nowhere." I hoped, but it was never said. The communication was comforting, but at the same time I knew deep down that it would be the last one with my girl on the Earth plane. I knew it wasn't going to be long, but I couldn't accept it. Her closing words still resonate. When asked if I was doing everything right for her, she replied, "Of course you are, my dear. You're doing everything perfectly." So ladylike, so much dignity, so Willow.'

'Goodbye, my Queen. I Love You'

Over Christmas and New Year Willow's health continued to slide. She spent most of her time on her special cushion, snuggled up and warm under a pink blanket. Jane would sit for hours stroking her and talking to her and Willow would blink slowly to acknowledge her. Her back legs had gone and she could hardly stand or walk. Then throughout one morning she was sick. Jane wrote:

'I held her over her litter tray to spare her dignity, as she hadn't the strength to get there herself. The vet took more bloods to ascertain whether it was her kidneys or whether her potassium was low, as this can happen in cats with renal failure. I knew in my heart that she wouldn't recover.

The day before her passing I sat with her and sobbed, because I felt the time was getting nearer. She stretched her paw out and placed it on my hand. Was she telling me, "Hey, don't worry, it'll be fine," or was she saying, "Let me go"?

The next morning I sat with her, kissed her and told her how special she was. She looked up from her cushion and our eyes met. I knew then she was telling me to let her go. I told her to stop fighting it and that I felt happy for her to leave me now. I gave her permission, as I knew it wasn't fair to expect her to stay any longer.

Our vet, Jason, rang later with the results and told me, "Her kidneys have totally failed." In less than a month they had gone from critical to total failure and he said there was nothing he could do. I asked him to visit us one last time. As I stroked Willow's head I noticed that it was wet from my tears. My final words to her were "Goodbye, my queen. I love you."'

Willow's body was carried out of the house wrapped in her pink blanket.

> *'The days that followed were horrendous. I cried a river, but deep, deep down I knew I had done the right thing. To see her staggering was probably harder than her passing. That wasn't the Willow I knew and loved, and that wasn't the Willow she wanted to be.'*

It was 5 January 2010 when Willow was assisted over. That day it began to snow, and it snowed and snowed until Gloucestershire was covered in a glorious gleaming blanket of purity, as if the Earth were being bathed in a magical glow ready for new life.

Willow's Advice from Beyond the Grave

When Jane contacted me a few weeks later, she was understandably still grieving. I connected with Willow and without prompting she immediately started to express herself in the same manner as before, except that her energy felt stronger and somehow more complete. She wanted to talk about Jane:

> *'She's a worrier. She can't help it. She worries about everything. My job was to calm her down and remind her how special she was. I did my job well. I can say this now I am on the other side of the physical reality.*
>
> *She is not supported enough by her husband. He doesn't understand how hard it is to juggle so many things – to divide the energy in so many different ways. He will one day fully comprehend.*
>
> *I am well and relaxed – no longer in pain lower down. My kidneys were in dire condition, especially my left – very sore, hopeless really. Jason is a kind man; he came to end*

my days. It was the right time. I was ready to go. I was very weak and could hardly walk. That was no kind of life for me.'

When I saw Willow in my mind's eye she was glowing with vitality, with lustrous fur. She continued with life advice for Jane:

'Tell Jane to slow down. She is working too hard and needs to give herself more time to unwind and play, to really enjoy herself. I want to see her laugh again. To smile and feel a lightness in her heart. To dance around the garden naked! To feel her full divine feminine essence. To harness her female power. I was always trying to remind her of the power she had, but I grew tired. Now I am at full strength again I will be more direct with my message.'

I was writing the message down and would type up every last word.

Willow continued, addressing Jane directly:

'Baby girl, stop trying to please everyone else and put yourself first. They will show you more love and respect if you do. Follow my example – didn't I always put myself first? Didn't I always draw others to me? This is not a selfish act, it is a self-ish act, putting the focus on your self – your soul being, physical being and emotional being. You know I care for you and say this with love in my heart, because our hearts are entwined. You have always done what's right for me; now I am trying to do what's right for you – will you let me? Will you listen?'

I was sure Jane would listen.

Jane had wanted to know whether Willow had passed over OK and who was taking care of her now. I put these questions to Willow.

'I was gone in an instant,' she replied, 'because I was ready to let go. It was what I wanted. And I take care of myself, because I am Willow. And a cat.'

Jane had asked whether she was ready to go.

'Yes, very ready. I urged you to let me go and you listened to my message. You were brave. And I am grateful.'

Jane had another cat called Blue who was the same age as Willow and had arrived on the same day. Although from a different litter, she had been like a sister to her. She also had health concerns now. Jane had asked whether Willow could tell her if Blue was OK.

Willow answered, 'Blue is getting tired. She has to rest more, but she is content for now. You don't need to worry about her. Just let her be, enjoying her life. She knows I am close. I have not left her, or you. You may feel my essence close by. Kisses. Head rubs.'

Jane's last question was: 'I felt Willow was my soul mate and wonder if she will ever come back to me?'

'Yes, we are soul mates,' Willow replied. 'Always connected. But I don't feel I want to come back as another body. I feel one lifetime together was perfect and irreplaceable and I was very happy with that physical body. I will wait until we are both back together and then we can reincarnate together. I hope that is OK with you.'

Later Jane wrote to me: 'I know those messages were from Willow because I always called her "baby girl" and in her message that's what she called me. Thank you.'

Blue

Blue stayed by Jane's side for another 12 months, just as Willow had done.

'That old ailing cat healed me through every anniversary,' she said.

The weekend before Blue passed over, Derek, a fulfilment manager of an online optical company, thought he saw Willow jump off Jane's lap. He described her as 'like a bright light, but the essence was Willow'.

Then the day before Blue died, Jane's sister was convinced she had seen Willow walking into Jane and Derek's bedroom.

Jane told me, 'To me, this was her final duty: Willow came back to help Blue across.'

It was reassuring to know that Willow had come to accompany Blue to the other side. It was also humbling to hear Willow giving life advice to Jane. If an animal is able to know so much about other animals, and people, both in their physical body and as souls who passed over many years earlier, it is exciting to think how much they could know about other areas of life, death and beyond.

In the next chapter I'd like to share with you how Morgan suddenly fell ill and how I begged him to stay with me a while longer. We will also look at the importance of palliative care and whether animals can decide whether to stay or go.

Chapter 3
Morgan, Master Teacher

⊙♥♥

'The journey is yours, you know the path.'
MORGAN

Morgan, as I mentioned earlier, wasn't actually perfect when he arrived. He had emotional blocks from his life before rescue and it took a little while to help him through these. He barked at every elderly man with a walking stick, desperate to get his attention. I'm sure he felt each of these men could be his previous guardian. There was also his desire to chase Texas, who really couldn't have been less impressed. Being of mainly beagle nature, Morgan was also greatly skilled at going deaf on recall, preferring to bound and bark through dense woodland after fox scents. It was only when silence fell that I would begin to worry. One time I was out with my partner and friends and their well-behaved, stick-to-your-side-like-glue golden retriever when Morgan disappeared for over 10 minutes. It was hard to ignore their looks of concern and disapproval. The four of us tried to cover every possible exit of the wood and eventually he came out trotting along with the biggest smile, not realizing that our blood pressure had soared sky-high while he was up to his capers.

Morgan also pulled hard on the lead at first, vacuumed up everything in sight and would virtually rip my arm out of the socket if he encountered a fox on a late-night walk, barking the whole street awake in his excitement. Not one to need physical affection, he would outsmart anyone reaching out to give him a friendly pat, manoeuvring away from outstretched fingers with utmost precision. He was healthy, active and stubborn as hell.

He was also sheer joy. Once he had let go of the past and had his paws firmly rooted to the sofa, he exuded self-contentment. He loved to be playful, though not with toys that he considered pointless. He'd only chase a ball if there was something in it, and that had to be food-related. His playfulness was different: he preferred to instigate running together, beaming a huge smile as he did so.

He came to teach at some of my animal communication workshops and was determined that every student in the room should experience some level of true connection. He could be anxious beforehand, but once in the room he was exemplary and touched many hearts. He also had great timing and knew to the minute when he was scheduled to teach, getting up and standing the other side of the door waiting to be let in.

He helped me with my clients' animals too – those in physical body, those missing and those who had transitioned. If I ever got a bit blocked, I'd simply ask Morgan for help and he'd give me an answer.

He could also help me understand confusing situations by revealing their essence. Humans have many veils, but animals can see past the hype to the truth of the situation. Morgan's finely tuned radar has helped me on many occasions when humans have tried to mislead or manipulate.

Everything was wonderful for five years and he was a huge blessing in my life, but then I began to get the feeling that something awful was about to happen to him.

'Do You Get Premonitions?'

This usually happened when Morgan and I were out walking together. I would feel the fear in my stomach, a heavy pit of dread. It happened time and again. I wanted to push the feeling away and kept telling myself, *No, he's fine, he's well and he'll be here for quite a while yet.* Having recently come to believe that our thoughts could be very influential, I wanted to remain positive.

On 14 January 2009 the feeling was too strong to ignore. There didn't seem to be a particular reason for it. Morgan had walked a bit funny when he'd got out of his bed in the morning, as if he had his sea legs on, but within 30 minutes or so he'd seemed to be more stable. He'd managed his morning walk without a hitch and eaten breakfast as usual. Nevertheless, during the walk I decided I'd have to make the call I'd been putting off for weeks.

Around 11 a.m. I rang my friend Lynne, the guardian of Riki, the Spinone dog who features in *Heart to Heart*. The main purpose of the call was to ask her if Morgan had said anything to her about his health. They'd always had a strong connection, even though physically they'd only ever met once. I knew Morgan trusted her.

I asked, 'Do you sense anything from Morgan about how he is feeling physically?'

'No, why?' she said.

'Oh, it's just this feeling I have. It won't go away. I've had it for weeks.'

'Do you get premonitions?' Lynne asked.

'Yes, occasionally. I just hope that this isn't one of them.'

Morgan was an older dog, but he wasn't frail. He was still running and enjoying life.

Literally as Lynne and I were talking about this, I was drawn to Morgan, who was lying beside me on the sofa. I didn't know what was happening straightaway.

'Something's wrong with Morgan,' I said.

'What do you mean?'

'He can't control his body, it's gone tense and his eyes are flicking manically from side to side. Something's not right.'

There was a moment's pause and then Lynne said very calmly, 'It sounds as though he could be having a stroke or seizure. Keep him calm and reassure him.'

I could feel his distress. 'OK, Morgan, you're all right,' I said to him gently. 'I'm with you. You're going to be fine.'

'Is he twitching or jerking? Make sure he can't hurt himself,' Lynne instructed.

'No, he's quite still and tense really. He's holding his head at a bizarre angle. He's on the sofa next to me and I can make sure he won't fall off.'

Morgan had no intention of moving off the sofa. He was suffering.

'What do you feel?' I asked him and I mentally tried to put myself inside his body.

He refused to let me in, but replied, 'Burning. Fire.'

I could see an area moving rapidly on the top of his head just behind his right eye. It was undulating, as though little volcanic explosions were happening just underneath the surface.

'What can I do?' I said to him.

But now Morgan was silent. He was in a different place. In the stroke. Experiencing the pain.

'Have you got any homoeopathic remedies?' Lynne asked.

'Yes, lots,' I replied.

She suggested some remedies that could help him. Thank goodness I was on the phone to Lynne! I hadn't experienced this before and didn't know what to do.

Even worse, I could feel Morgan going further and further away from me. Lynne and I decided to hang up so I could put all my focus on Morgan. I wanted to channel healing to him, speak to him and reassure him that everything would be OK.

I kneeled on the floor in front of the sofa, cradling his head in my hands. I looked into his eyes, but they were still darting from left to right and back again. Tears streamed down my face. I could feel I was losing him.

'Morgan, I love you. I love you and I'm not ready to let you go yet. I need you to stay. I want you to stay here with me, OK?'

I couldn't feel if Morgan was connecting with my words, so I carried on saying them.

'I'm not ready to let you go, Morgan. I need you to stay. It's too soon. I want more time with you.'

Then I sensed his spirit hovering up in the air out of his body.

'*Please* stay with me, Morgan, just for a little longer,' I pleaded, as tears burned my cheeks.

While keeping an eye on him to make sure he couldn't fall and hurt himself, I reached for the phone. Within minutes I was listening to the very soothing and sympathetic voice of veterinarian homoeopath Richard Allport. He prescribed some remedies, instructed me on dosage and explained that with good nursing care many dogs were able to work through strokes.

'What does that mean, "good nursing care"?' I said.

'It really means being there for them. Supporting them and waiting to see what happens.'

I knew I could be there for Morgan. I also knew I needed to be positive while waiting to see whether he had the strength to recover.

While I was cradling his head, I heard him say: 'Mackerel.'

I knew this was important because Morgan was mostly a one-word dog. I'd make sure I got him some mackerel if that was what he felt he needed.

I grabbed the drawer full of homoeopathic remedies and scattered them across the rug to discover I didn't have the specific remedies in the correct strength. I would be able to begin giving them in a weaker strength, but this wouldn't be enough.

I rang my friend Jenny, who adored Morgan and lived close by, but only reached her answerphone. This time I was not so controlled as the truth of the situation hit me. I struggled to sputter out: 'Morgan is having a stroke. I need some homoeopathic remedies *really* quickly. Jo is away and I can't leave him. Can you help? He also wants mackerel. Please ring me back.'

Next I rang my partner, Jo, who was on a train to Leeds. She was in work mode, thinking about her lighting design for her upcoming show, and it took a couple of calls to get across the severity of the situation.

'He's really not well. I don't know what's going to happen,' I reiterated.

Jo caught the next train back home.

Time ticked on slowly while I held Morgan, gently stroked his head and tried to take control of my emotions. His eyes continued to dart and the top of his head to bubble. I was so worried for him. He looked so vulnerable.

It felt like eternity before I heard from Jenny, even though it was less than 20 minutes in reality.

'Sorry, Pea, I had no phone signal. How is he? What do you need?'

Over the next hour I was able to calm myself and give Morgan homoeopathic remedies at 10-minute intervals as instructed. I also channelled Reiki healing energy. I was thankful that I'd trained to Master level. I could feel he was struggling. Although he wasn't communicating his thoughts to me, instinctively I knew I needed to stay by his side with my hand touching him so he could feel my presence.

Then Jenny arrived and I was able to give Morgan the stronger remedies. She spoke sweet soft words to him and gently stroked his side. It was such a support having someone in the house who was calm and soothing. Very soon her partner, Tony, joined us too, loaded with varieties of mackerel.

I offered Morgan the mackerel, but he didn't take it. He'd lost the use of his neck and his head was at a very acute angle to the left. I tried him with some coley, but he didn't take that either. It was hard to see this, because food was always the one thing that could be guaranteed to get his interest.

Looking back, I feel those early hours of care were crucial. I kept a notepad to hand and wrote down every time I gave Morgan the remedies to make sure I wasn't missing a dose. It was amazing how time would just slip by. Before we knew it, the next dose would be due. I continued to offer him the mackerel, too, and finally he took some from my hand. It was only a tiny amount, but it gave me hope.

Over the next four hours I felt he was making steady progress. He ate mackerel on and off, and started to look more relaxed. I could feel myself relaxing too. Morgan's eyes were still very glazed over, but the feeling of confusion had lessened. With every glimmer of recovery, I had more hope that he was fighting his way back to me.

Remedies and care continued all afternoon and Jo made it home. Texas remained absent; maybe he knew it wasn't a good time to come back.

A little later, Morgan's eyes stopped flicking and finally came to rest.

In the early evening he tried to get off the sofa. His head was still strongly angled and he couldn't stand by himself. Some dogs will allow you to support them with towels underneath their body, but not Morgan. We tried his soft fleece harness instead and he accepted this.

Thankfully, he was able to toilet. You might not think this counts for much, but we were delighted that this bodily function was working OK.

As it began to grow dark outside, Morgan was keen to go out of the front door. He had always been a very determined dog and once he'd made his mind up about something it was very hard to change it, so we opened the door and supported him over the threshold and through the creaky wooden gate. He marched off – insofar as you can march when you're being held up by your bright yellow fluorescent harness and have little control over your direction – and made it three houses up the road before he was ready to go back. It was another cause for celebration. His inner routine was still there and would help him pull through. Most dogs love routine and Morgan was no exception.

Later that evening our friends headed home and Jo and I turned the sofa into a makeshift bed so we could do shifts and give Morgan round-the-clock care. I am convinced that animals know we are by their side supporting them even if they don't outwardly show it. If we are able to be calm and positive when we're with them, this energy can have a positive influence on their recovery.

Texas returned home and from his face it was obvious he knew Morgan wasn't right. He kept his distance and an uncharacteristic low profile – no cries for food, no requests to be let out or back in, no waking us up, no demands at all. He virtually vanished into the shadows.

I took the first shift and lay on the sofa watching Morgan doze in his bed. I felt wiped out by the day's emotion and found it a struggle to stay awake. Morgan's breathing was heavy and erratic. He wasn't settled. He was going on his own journey now. Only time would tell if he could get through this, if there would be lasting damage affecting his future or if, by some miracle, he could make it back to his former self.

By the time Jo took over at 5 a.m., I was feeling sick with tiredness. When I came back down about 9 a.m., I found Jo and Morgan cuddled together on the sofa. He'd had mainly quiet hours and no more dramas.

15 January 2009, Day 2: Custard Tarts

Our allopathic vet looks into Morgan's eyes, gives him a general exam, concludes he's had a stroke and prescribes some medicine. We discover it primarily contains omega-3 fats, which help provide fluidity to brain cell membranes, improving communication between the cells, and are essential for efficient brain function. The mackerel Morgan requested is also high in omega-3 and it is clear to me that he knew what he needed to make himself well again.

I break down in tears standing in front of the receptionist's desk fumbling to pay the bill. Despite the fact that Morgan is now wobbling along with support, for some reason it has upset me to receive this concrete diagnosis.

At lunch I speak to our holistic vet again and he tweaks the prescription. Jo and I decide to leave the allopathic medicine in the drawer as back-up and continue with the homoeopathy instead. Morgan hasn't reacted too well to mainstream medicine in the past and has seemed to do much better on something holistic. This is not to say we'd turn our back on allopathic medicine completely, as everything has a time and place and it can be brilliant for emergency treatment. But in this case we are looking at a dog who has already begun to recover and needs long-term support.

Morgan is still very tense in his neck and struggling to hold his head up. Physically, he is exhausted. I am wondering if there is anything else I can do to help him…

Our Spinone friend is quick to connect and tell me, 'Give him a custard tart.'

Jo races off to the supermarket and stocks up. The tarts are the only food to pique Morgan's interest; over the course of the day he accepts being hand fed three of them. The boost of egg and sugar will give him energy while his body is engaged in repairing itself.

We decide to make life more comfortable for him and place the double mattress from our guest room on the living-room floor along with a couple of covers and a soft duvet. Morgan happily sets up camp there and visibly relaxes. We help create a healing environment by keeping the lights low and the room warm and quiet. It is now possible to leave the room knowing that if Morgan wants to try to get up to follow us he won't fall far or hurt himself.

Sometimes he is unsure where he is or what he's doing, and when we call him he looks in the wrong direction. He is unable to close his right eye, so we bathe it with eyewashes to avoid it becoming dry and sore.

When I ask him, 'Do you know what's happened?' he replies, 'Explosion in my head.'

16 January, Day 3: Progress

Morgan manages to jump onto the sofa next to me. How did he do that? It's remarkable what he can achieve even when his body is shattered. He also makes the decision to go to the kitchen in search of his food bowls, marching off like a puppet on strings. He uses the wall for support some of the way and we hold him up by his harness for the rest.

In the evening we watch as he staggers like a good drunk out onto the grass completely unaided – just as he wants it. My heart soars because I know he is determined to carry on.

17 January, Day 4: Panting Zombie

Morgan's head is still at a very acute angle, but with the assistance of the wall he makes it all the way to the front door to greet Jenny and Tony, who have come to see how he is doing.

However, he is off his food and keeps waking up and panting excessively. Once his paws are on the cool green grass of the garden he'll urinate for England and the panting will abruptly stop.

His bowel movements aren't good either and there is a moment outside when he is totally unaware of what he is doing. I guide him back by talking softly to him.

I think because he has been able to perform daily functions such as walking, toileting and eating so soon it has been easy to forget that the important recovery is taking place inside his head.

18 January, Day 5: Toxic Meltdown

Morgan wakes up stronger and more relaxed. But later he loses his appetite and his bodily functions go into meltdown with a long period of bright yellow diarrhoea. Is this toxins being released from the chemical reactions of the stroke?

He curls up tightly and squeezes himself into Texas's rectangular burgundy bed, the one with the wording on the front: 'Do Not Disturb'. He could not make it clearer.

Thankfully, by evening his tummy has settled and he is smiling from his own bed.

Then something wonderful happens – Texas starts to be vocal. For nearly five whole days he has acted completely against character and faded silently into the shadows. We take this as a very positive sign that everything is getting back to normal.

19 January, Day 6: Granny's Funeral and a Ritz Biscuit

I have to leave Morgan. It is my granny's funeral. I will attend by myself while Jo stays and cares for him.

I return feeling depressed, but a very simple thing changes my mood completely: on the evening walk Morgan pulls me by his lead in order to reach a discarded Ritz biscuit on the street. This small gesture of normality makes me laugh out loud.

20 January, Day 7: Morgan's Return

Seven days after his stroke the clouded gaze lifts and Morgan returns, his eyes bright, sparkling with sunshine. I look into those

*chocolate-coloured depths and his soul essence looks lovingly
back at me.*

'You're back, sweetheart,' I say.

His eyes smile.

Choosing More Life

Morgan now started to make great improvements every day. He
could walk more by himself and began to eat without help. He
still preferred to have us in his sight, but a lot of his day was taken
up in sleeping, except in the afternoon when there was a daily
release of toxins, with less each time and a quicker recovery.

He'd been receiving support through communication, healing,
lit candles and positive thoughts, which I am sure helped him a
lot, but I believe in the end it was his incredible determination
that saw his return to us. He *chose* more life.

Up until his stroke Morgan had always been independent and
happy to sleep downstairs in the living room at night. But afterwards
Jo and I decided to move his bed to our room so if anything happened
in the night we would be close and able to react quickly.

As time passed, Morgan began to be much more his old self.
Jo and I drove him to the bottom of the road one day so he could
walk round his local woods without the restriction of a lead. He
was thrilled, wagged his tail the whole time and in fact walked us
round. He was beaming with happiness. I feel some woods hold a
kind of magic that can heal animals on a deeper level.

The following day, one hour before his usual walk time
Morgan insisted that we go to the woods. I surrendered to his
demand and we headed off at a steady pace for a boost of nature's
healing energy. I later realized it was the only time all day when
the sun was shining.

On the walk back a dishevelled-looking old man shuffling
along the pavement pointed to Morgan's fluorescent harness and
asked if he was in training.

Morgan stopped by a tree for a sniff and I answered, 'No, it's because he's a bit wobbly.'

The stranger said, 'He's all right. God bless him. He's all right. All the best to him. He won't hear me, but all the best to him.'

'He'll hear you,' I said, smiling, thinking *If only you knew*.

The man giggled, 'All the best to him. He's good as gold. He's all right. Look, he's wagging his tail.'

I looked at Morgan and he was wagging his tail.

'All the best to him,' the man repeated.

'Thank you,' I said, touched by his kindness.

'All the best to you too. God bless you. God bless you both,' he said.

Morgan and I continued home with the old man shuffling down the pavement behind us. As we were about to round the corner, I glanced back to wave goodbye, but he'd completely disappeared. I looked all around but he was nowhere to be seen. Within the space of 10 yards he'd completely vanished.

The stranger didn't know that one of my stock phrases to Morgan was 'you're good as gold'. It felt as though he was a messenger giving me a sign that all was well.

Did he know Morgan could hear him?

Morgan's Prediction

The sky was blue and everywhere was quiet when Morgan made his prediction. He was lying in his tartan-patterned oval bed in the living room and I was sitting on the sofa opposite him.

'Thank you so much for staying with me,' I said, thinking back to when I felt he was drifting away from me.

He raised his head, looked directly into my eyes and in a matter-of-fact tone I heard him state: 'Two years.'

I knew what he meant straightaway: he was telling me he planned on staying two more years and then his current lifetime would come to an end and he would let go.

Sometime later I told Jo that Morgan had given me his predicted lifetime and as I expected, she didn't want to know. I respected her decision. Morgan and I would keep it our little secret.

Two more years, I thought to myself. *Then we'd better make them the best two years ever.*

Do animals know what lies ahead for them? In the next chapter, the guardian of BeBe Begonia, a 15-year-old black cat diagnosed with lymphoma and priapism, asked, 'Does he know how sick he is?' and 'Does he want us to aid his death or does he want to go through the entire process on his own?'

Chapter 4
BeBe Begonia, Love Cat

೪

*'Do not worry about me when I am gone
and on the other side. Life is eternal.'*
BEBE BEGONIA

When Ellen contacted me from New York she wanted to hear first-hand from her shorthaired soot-black 15-year-old moggy, BeBe Begonia.

Ellen had taken BeBe in as a tiny kitten even before he was weaned and walking. Her husband, David, had seen a sign stapled to a telephone pole: 'Homes Needed for Kittens.' The litter of seven had been born to a sleek and beautiful feral mother cat between two buildings in New York City. Someone had provided a box for her to give birth in, but when some of the kittens began to walk they were in danger. They needed homes.

When BeBe was still very young, Ellen kept hearing the word *bébé*, French for 'baby', complete with French accent. She wanted the new kitten to carry on the legacy of a previous cat she had had called Egypt Begonia, so she added 'Begonia', and that's how the kitten was named BeBe Begonia.

At the time Ellen approached me she was distraught. She'd experienced the passing of her friends, her father, her sister and the loss of a pre-adoptive baby and other four-legged animal loves, yet she described the approaching loss of BeBe as all of those other losses rolled into one.

When I looked at BeBe's photo, I found myself gazing at a very sleek and slim cat standing facing the camera with his head at a quizzical angle and both front paws together in first position as if waiting to choreograph the next stage of a ballet. There was a heart-shaped identity tag dangling from his neck like a medallion. But I was to discover BeBe was far from the 'medallion man' of the seventies – he was much more sophisticated.

BeBe had suffered from a variety of ailments over the past few years: fatty liver disease, severe constipation and lymphoma. He had recovered from the liver disease and was responding excellently to the treatment for lymphoma.

Ellen said, 'In the previous few years, he has been sick on and off and badly misunderstood and misdiagnosed. Thankfully, he has always come through, resuming his habits, games and rituals.'

BeBe had now been diagnosed with priapism, otherwise known as constant erection, a painful and irreversible problem.

'He's had it for a few weeks and I'm told the only cure is a sex-change operation,' Ellen told me. 'It could be caused by the lymphoma or it could be from a stroke. When he walks he needs to swing his right rear leg out to the side to avoid rubbing against his member.'

I could only imagine how awful it must be for BeBe.

'Due to his age, his lymphoma and the exorbitant cost, he's not a candidate for the sex-change operation,' Ellen explained. 'Even if he were, I wouldn't subject him to it. But untreated, priapism causes lethal infections and strokes, so again it's just a matter of time. I'm not going to wait for either of those possibilities. He's so unhappy and so uncomfortable, and I feel his quality of life has diminished more than during any previous ailments. I need to know his wishes. Does he know how sick he is? Does he want us to aid his death? Or does he want to go through the entire process on his own? And, if he wants help, how will I know when he is ready?'

It was time to begin communicating with BeBe. I needed to be very neutral and give him space to express whatever he wished without any judgement of my own.

I looked gently into his gold eyes and went through my process of connecting, then began to list the impressions I was receiving:

'Stoical cat. Not one to complain.
His hips are a problem. He walks stiffly, but does enjoy going out.
Lives with three others.
He's finding it difficult to eat.'

The list was very short. BeBe wasn't interested in small talk; he wanted to get straight to the point and answer Ellen's questions. Despite being very unwell, he was confident and direct.

I began, 'Ellen wishes to know whether you're aware how sick you are.'

'Yes, more than she is,' he replied. His voice in my mind had a deep tone and there was wisdom running through it.

'Do you want her to aid your death or do you wish to go through the entire process on your own?'

'Now is not the time. Not until later,' he said.

This sounded hopeful. If BeBe felt it was not his time to go then he must also be aware that he could carry on.

'If you need Ellen's help in the future, how will she know that you're ready?' I said.

'She will know. I will look at her and she will know. I will be still, not getting up. At the moment I still have some joy in life.'

This sounded so much more positive than the scenario Ellen had given me based on the diagnosis and BeBe's external behaviour.

'Ellen wants to know what you need from her to make it easier for you to go,' I said to him.

'Love and patience. All the best qualities in a human, which you have in abundance.'

Ellen had asked, 'Does he know he means the world to me?'

He replied directly to her, 'Yes, my dear, and you to me. I have always loved you.' He spoke with a mature air.

'I want him to know that he doesn't need to hang around suffering on my behalf.'

'I am not suffering as you think I am. The outside is but a shell. It's what's on the inside that counts.'

'Does he want to continue the medications that are keeping his body working for now?'

'Yes, in smaller doses,' BeBe replied. He felt they were too strong for him.

'Does he want pain medicine?'

'Yes, all the time,' he replied insistently. 'It is my back which is sorest.' He went on to request some gentle massage movements too.

'What would he like David, Angie and me to know?'

At this point I had no idea whether David and Angie were human family, cats or other animals, so I waited to see what BeBe would say.

When he delivered his message for David, it was one of emotion. I could feel BeBe had a great fondness for what turned out to be a man. It seemed they were kindred spirits.

'Sweet Angie,' he continued. 'You still have a lot to learn, but I am very proud of you. Don't cry over me.'

Ellen said, 'Although our daughter did cry when she heard this, I believe it helped her. We adopted her when she was nine.

She has many emotional issues to heal from and I think knowing BeBe's view of her touched her.'

BeBe ended with: 'Ellen, do not worry about me when I am gone and on the other side. Life is eternal and I will be back to see you again. Our companionship is not over. I will reincarnate. You will know me. I will be a very tiny kitten once more.'

Afterwards Ellen e-mailed:

> *'Thank you so much, Pea. The communication... has given me the confidence to not end BeBe's life, even though friends, family, and vets are telling me "it is time" or "it's been time for a while". I have begun to trust my instincts and I trust I will know when and that BeBe will help me know.'*

Priapism No More

I was so excited to receive the next e-mail from Ellen just eleven days later:

> *'BeBe's priapism reversed itself last week.'*

This was less than two weeks after he'd communicated that he wasn't ready to pass over and wanted to wait. Had he known that he would recover from this condition? Was he aware he'd get better despite the veterinary prognosis that he'd only live for one or two weeks at most? And despite strong advice from vets and friends that it was time to let him go?

Ellen continued:

> *'He is now able to pee and poop without medications and the lymphoma wound on his leg has started healing. Already two of the four medications have been eliminated. He is much happier and no longer at death's door. I do believe that the opportunity to communicate helped him.'*

I was so thrilled. This was the best sort of news.

Ellen added:

> *'Due to the extraordinary changes in BeBe's health, may*
> *I get one more insight? I didn't bring it up before because*
> *I was led to believe that BeBe would die in the next week*
> *or two. I need to be out of town for a job and I'll be gone*
> *two and a half weeks. I want to hear whether he will be*
> *OK during my absence. It's too late for me to back out of it*
> *and I want to leave making sure he knows what's going on*
> *and that I will be back. My husband and daughter will be*
> *at home with him, but I don't want him to feel abandoned*
> *by me.'*

Three and a half weeks after his first communication, BeBe was still alive and I was linking in with him again.

He began, 'I am still strong.'

'I'm so glad you're feeling much better,' I told him. 'Ellen has some more questions and messages for you.'

'I am ready,' he said.

Ellen asked, 'How is he feeling now? Any better? In pain?'

He said, 'I feel sore in my abdomen.'

'What does he want or need?'

'He's asking for more plain chicken rather than biscuits,' I passed on. 'Something that is easier to digest. He also wants more warmth.'

'I love the sunshine,' BeBe added.

'I want to know what will help him while I am gone,' Ellen said.

'Hearing from you daily,' BeBe decided.

'Can he cooperate with David by taking his medicine with minimum biting and scratching? Please let him know how much I've appreciated his cooperation.'

'BeBe finds it hard to accept the medicine. He will try and relax. Can David use the word "relax" when he's giving BeBe the medicine? It might help them both.'

'I would like him to know that I will be away for two and a half weeks from June 27ᵗʰ and I am coming back.'

'Yes, I know,' he replied. 'I'm not happy about it, but I accept it. I will miss you every day. Talk to me often.'

'Is there anything else he wants to share?'

'Do not worry about me, not even for a moment. You know I will be all right. I am strong, and David is here and he loves me, and Angie too. There is a lot of love in this house. I am very proud of you all. I will wait until you come home.'

'I know he already knows how deeply I love and value him,' Ellen said to me, 'but it can't hurt to tell him.'

I did so and BeBe ended the communication by saying to Ellen, 'I love you to the moon and stars and back. Never forget this.'

Ellen went on her work trip and it was another year before I heard from her again.

The Perfect Time

Ellen wrote:

I just want you to know that BeBe has now passed away. He lived for an additional year after the priapism episode and the implication that he was about to die. As he told you, he was stronger then I knew and continued to live and love life.

I spent four years keeping his death at bay. He let me. He cooperated – recovering from illnesses, ending a hunger strike, swallowing medication, and responding to chemo. He continued chemo treatments every six weeks with the oncology vet and his wound stayed closed. When he developed trouble breathing, he went back to the regular vet, who said it was probably the cancer. The oncology vet said his cancer was under control and it was heart disease. Either way, the answer was the same: there was nothing they could do to help.

Over our extra year he gave me time to sort through my feelings and get to the bottom of my sorrow. I dug down to the bottom of the pain and found it to be a lifelong sadness that I had not been loved the way I wanted to be loved. Even if it was a childish, unrealistic expectation, I still had the sorrow. I know BeBe and I were soul mates and we had a deep connection. His love was perfect for me; it was healing my unresolved wound. To me, he was a divine being in his simple, deeply present way.

I released him from caring for me. I let him know that I was going to be OK and he should use all of his strength for himself. After this, he stopped sleeping on my pillow. A few months later he stopped coming in while I bathed. Then he stopped coming to the door when I came home.

His lungs became full of fluid, leaving him gasping for breath and unable to eat or drink. I knew it was time to let him go. But I was also in denial. After all, he'd recovered all the other times, why not this time? But the X-ray revealed an untreatable situation. No new medicine, no hope, just the suggestion that I take him home, say goodbye, and bring him back tomorrow.

I took their latest appointment for the following evening and carried him home. We spent the afternoon quietly on the sofa and I sat with him through the night.

In the morning, I went out back to the hammock with a blanket and pillow, trusting he would follow. When he did, I lifted him up and we napped. Later he ate a meal and then jumped up onto the bed, so I cancelled the appointment and took the latest one for the following day. But after sitting with him day and night and again the next day, I cancelled the appointment and made one for the day after that.

I had hope... I had hope all day Friday, all day Saturday, all day Sunday, and hope until 3:30 p.m. on Monday when BeBe started to pant and a small strand of drool hung from the corner of his usually dainty mouth.

He finally gave me the signal that he was ready. I knew it was the exact right moment. Just as he told you, he looked at me and he did not move. We just looked at each other from across the room and I could see so clearly, he was showing me without a doubt that he needed to leave. His look gave me the courage to do it. Even sick and weak, he was commanding in his presence. I will never forget that look in his eyes – how revealing it was. It was the first time he was completely separate from me.

I called the vet's office and took the next available appointment: 5:30 p.m.

At 5:30 p.m. the vet was busy with an emergency... It was the first time I was happy to wait an hour and a half for an appointment because BeBe and I were still together. I knew it was my responsibility to end his suffering. Others had been encouraging me to do it for days, weeks, and some for years. But I knew that yesterday was too soon, that this morning was too soon. I knew that this was the time.

The vet came in and gave him a pre-euthanizing sedative while he lay in my arms. I held him and silently told him what I've told him so many times on my pillow, on the sofa, in the hammock, and on buses and trains: "I love you, BeBe. Don't worry, you're safe. As long as we are together, you are safe."

Then he passed away. He was dead before the lethal injection. It was time. It was his time. It was the only time. The perfect time.'

Through my communications with animals I've come to realize that some animals stop eating when they are in pain and appear to be dying. At this point, instead of receiving pain-relief, they are euthanized. This is when assisted death is not in their best interests. With pain-relief, animals can sometimes recover their appetite and zest for life again.

On the flip side of this, pain can point to when an animal is suffering and no longer enjoying life. If the medication no longer relieves the pain, would they rather transition?

In deciding when an animal has had enough, surely it's helpful to ask the animal? By communicating with them, we allow them to tell us when it's the right time, just as BeBe knew it wasn't his time to transition and a week later his 'irreversible' and 'fatal' priapism reversed itself and he lived for another year. If a communication is linked with advice from a trusted veterinarian who knows the animal well and the guardian's own gut feeling, it is possible for the right decision to be reached at the right time.

When we face the death of a beloved animal friend, one question that often comes to mind is: *Are you holding on for me?* In the next chapter we'll look at what happened when Anna was told her cat, Benny, only had a month to live.

Part II
FACING DEATH WITH GRACE

'In order to learn the art of dying, one must know completely the art of living.'
SATYA NARAYAN GOENKA

Chapter 5
Mi Amore Benny

⤜⤏

*'Death is an adventure into the next life and
also a letting-go of those we love in this life.
Death can be beautiful if we see it differently.'*
BENNY

Benny came into Anna's life when she put out a plea to the universe for a cat like her previous one. A short time later a dejected-looking black-and-white moggy walked in through her open office door, strolled around the counter, looked her straight in the face and jumped onto her lap and lay down. He was filthy dirty and his eyes were in a very bad state, but he burst into a symphony of purrs. His arrival was the beginning of a love story.

It was June 2010 when I first came across Anna and Benny. Anna was a 58-year-old computer-phobic Englishwoman living in northern Italy with her Italian husband, Mimmo. Her adult son and daughter were living away at the time.

But this story doesn't begin there: it starts 15 years earlier. At that time Anna had a cat called Sammy, a pure charcoal year-old beauty who was independent and not one for a lot of fuss and nonsense. Anna thought, *Wouldn't it be nice to have an affectionate cat like my parents' cat?* The next day Benny walked into her life.

Benny was very trusting right from the start and continued to purr as he lay on her lap while she drove to the vet.

'He exuded calm and happiness, looking up at me with so much love and trust that it went straight to my heart,' she said.

The vet lifted up the skin of Benny's sore eyes, but still the purring continued.

'I can't hear his heart because he's purring so loudly!' he exclaimed.

He diagnosed herpes virus, possibly transmitted by the mother. He also wanted to operate on Benny's left eye, which subsequently had to be removed. Thankfully, tests came back negative for other conditions and Anna was happy to take Benny home to her apartment, where she kept him hidden from sight.

'I didn't tell my husband straightaway. I knew he wouldn't want me to have another cat, but I did promise Benny, *I'll never throw you out. You'll always be with me.*'

It was a month later, when Benny was stronger, that Anna came clean and showed her husband the new arrival.

'Before he saw Benny that evening I asked him if he remembered the cat who had come into my office. He did and wanted to know what had happened to him. When I said he was at the vet's, he replied, "What a shame. If Sammy had accepted him, we could have kept him." That's when I said, "She *has*!"'

There was a deep understanding between Benny and Anna. 'Every night at around 11 o'clock he would come to me with a look in his eye and I knew what he wanted. I would say, "*Andiamo*," which means "Let's go" in Italian, and he would run into my bedroom and jump onto my bed.'

It didn't matter whether Anna spoke in Italian or English, bilingual Benny always understood. Of course, in reality he was receiving the energetic detail within the verbal words.

'I think he was almost like a dog,' Anna told me. 'Whenever I threw his soft ball he would bring it back to me, so excited he looked as though he was grinning. He was also so gentle – he never bit or scratched – and he was quiet. Sometimes I thought he didn't have a voice.'

Benny's arrival occurred just when he and Anna needed each other: she supported him through the loss of his eye and back from the brink of death, and he gave her the strength to carry on during the most difficult times of her life, when her daughter suffered deep depression and her son had an accident and nearly died.

He was especially attentive when people were sick, particularly when Anna was hospitalized with hepatitis caused by an allergic reaction to medication. At home she was in bed for over a week and he never left her side. He even followed her into the bathroom. Wherever she was, Benny would be there too. And when her black-nosed white rabbit, Nosely, was ill, Benny chose to sit with him for most of the day too.

'I realized,' Anna confessed, 'that Benny was therapeutic.'

In December 2008, when Anna was visiting her parents in England, she suddenly woke at 5 a.m. with a terrible feeling of dread.

'My thoughts were of Benny. I knew instinctively that something was seriously wrong and phoned home to check. I was reassured that all was well, but in February the following year Benny started to lose weight and was often sick. The vet diagnosed problems with his thyroid and prescribed medication, but he continued to lose weight, so I sought a second opinion. After more tests and a further wait, my premonition came true: he was diagnosed with cancer. The prognosis was not good: he was given one month to live. I was devastated. I knew then that Benny's cancer had started back in December.'

Benny was prescribed a steroid injection and over the next four weeks he stopped being sick and his appetite improved. Anna discovered that he loved wafer-thin raw meat and he gradually began to put on weight. When she took him back for a second steroid injection, the vet was amazed by how well he was responding to treatment. He continued to receive an injection at monthly intervals. Every now and then he would be sick, but his weight improved. Despite being given just one month to live, he was still with Anna 12 months later.

In need of a break, Anna and her husband went to England to visit her family.

'My dad had a surprise for me. It was a book called Heart to Heart *by Pea Horsley. He'd read about it in the* Daily Mail *and thought I would enjoy it. What he didn't realize, and neither did I, was just how important it would become to me. I devoured the book whilst I was on holiday. I must have looked so silly sitting under the umbrella on the beach crying my eyes out. I think there is a reason for everything and things are meant to be. I know now that I was meant to read it.'*

Thirteen months after he was given a month to live Benny had gained more weight and was looking good. The vet scanned him and discovered the tumour had disappeared.

'The injections were stopped immediately and I was very happy, but then as the weeks passed my instinct told me that something was seriously wrong. Each time I looked at Benny I just had this awful feeling of dread again.

At home I kept thinking about Pea communicating with animals. I knew it was real – I just had to pluck up the courage to call her. I was so worried about Benny – he looked tired and walked very slowly as though he was in pain. When I picked him up and gently stroked him, he didn't purr, and he always purred.

My sister gave me Pea's number in England. I felt nervous, but I knew I had to speak to her. My heart sank when there was no answer. Disappointed, I left my details on her voicemail. Ending the call, I turned around and discovered Benny staring up at me with a penetrating look on his adorable teddy-bear face. A connection was there and in my mind there was an urgency to try again, almost as if he was telling me to do so. I had the overwhelming feeling that he was dying.

I immediately rang back and began to leave another message on the answerphone – "Pea, I think he's dying" – and in that instant she picked up and spoke to me. Her voice was so reassuring. She asked me not to tell her anything about Benny, but to write down 10 questions and to e-mail them to her along with Benny's photo.'

Meeting Benny

It was May 2010 when I ran from the other end of the house to answer the call from Anna. I could hear her genuine distress and sense her deep love for Benny as she cried down the phone and I knew I wanted to help.

Sitting holding Benny's image, I found myself looking into the face of a sorrowful-looking cat. He was a hotchpotch of black and white in the oddest places. Jet black enveloped his ears and the top of his head then trailed down to a sharp point just where the inner side of his left eye would have been and diagonally down across his left cheek. He had a black nose with a diagonal black smudge at the same angle as the black on his cheek. With erratic black splodges and stripes on his legs, a banana-split half-white half-black tail and strong-looking black chin, he looked as if Picasso had been trying out a new design. However, his image didn't strike me as sorrowful for long.

Once I got myself quiet and reached out energetically to connect with Benny I came to understand he was much stronger in himself than I thought – not so much physically, but he had a presence. He felt physically fragile, just skin and bones, and he found his food smelled bad. He showed me an image of a dangly toy he used to love to play with, followed by an image of snuggling up with Anna on her bed, which I felt he loved. He showed me that he would purr when Anna stroked him, but he was only really interested in sleeping right now.

Anna verified these and other first impressions and we arranged a telephone appointment.

Anna wanted to ask Benny, 'How are you feeling?'

'He feels very sore, particularly his stomach area. It feels as though there's something in his stomach and there is a resonance of cancer. He aches all over and his mouth feels sore too. This problem causes him to be sick and to feel sick, so he finds it hard to eat.'

I didn't want to say any of this, but I knew Anna only wanted the truth and the whole truth.

'He was diagnosed with cancer two years ago,' she told me. 'The intestines were the main area affected... He used to love food. He used to come into the kitchen when I was cooking dinner. He used to love treats too, but now he's not eating much at all, just tiny bits of wafer-thin raw meat. What can I do to help him?'

I let her know Benny had requested a trip to the vet. He'd also suggested blood screening. He wasn't ready to die yet.

'Can you give me a sign to indicate you're communicating with me?' Anna asked him.

'Feel it in your heart,' Benny replied. 'I speak loudly to you.'

'Is there anything you would like me to do?' Anna prompted.

'I need urgent medical help. Steroids to help stimulate my appetite. Prepare for me to die,' he instructed. 'I would prefer to die calmly.'

Anna burst into tears, 'I knew it. I felt he was dying. I don't want him to suffer. He has been preparing me this whole year. I love him so much, he enters every fibre of my being. He's my soul mate.'

Equipped with all the information she wanted, she ended the call and went about phoning the vet for an appointment.

The vet confirmed Benny's stomach was sore because it was filled with fluid and his cancer was still present. The steroid injections were restarted immediately and within a few days Benny looked brighter in himself and was eating again.

But it wasn't to last. Anna's parents had visited for a couple of weeks and during the time it had taken to drop them at the airport, Benny had vomited a lot of liquid on the bedroom floor. From then on he went completely off his food and later that night he had a runny tummy and began to look very ill.

Anna rang me the next morning. 'How is he feeling?'

I sat still and quiet for a few minutes and linked in with Benny by looking gently into his one remaining eye, tuning in with his essence by immersing myself in his whole face.

He wasted no time in telling me, 'I'm very tired, Pea.'

I got straight to the important question: 'Is this your time to ascend?'

'No, not yet,' he replied, frankly.

'Why not?' I gently prompted. I wanted to be certain this was for his highest good.

'Because there is longer. The surface is deceptive,' he said.

'Everything tastes wrong to him,' I reported back to Anna. 'He loves lying on your bed. His mouth is sore and his limbs are heavy; it's an effort to move. He showed blackness around his heart. It feels as though he needs to drink to regulate his temperature. But he would like another injection, because he says it's not his time to go. He is not ready to ascend.'

Anna felt relieved, but deep down her heart was breaking at the thought of losing him: *Not yet, Benny. Not yet, darling.*

I relayed Benny's next message to her: 'Be prepared for losing me – the physical me – but know I am always around you. We can continue to love one another from a distance – physical distance, not emotional. You are my everything. Never forget this, sweet angel. I have brought some balance into your life. Focus on this – the balance. Remember this – it's important.'

'He has – he has brought some balance,' Anna reflected. 'I've had quite serious things happen where I've needed to be strong for others, and he's got me through it. Please ask him if there's anything that he's not happy about.'

'The pain,' Benny answered. 'Discomfort and feeling odd. But I am learning to meditate away from it. I feel very fragile and I do not like this feeling, because you know that I am not fragile.'

I asked him, 'How do you feel emotionally?'

'Preparing – preparing for the end of this lifetime.'

'Is there anything particular he wants to eat?' Anna said.

He showed an image of something like fresh ham and Anna told me she'd been feeding him very finely sliced veal for the past year. She told me she'd continue offering it to him, then asked, 'Does he want to see the vet for another steroid injection?'

'Yes. It's not time yet,' he said, referring to his transition.

'Is there anything he wants to tell me?'

Benny said, 'Never underestimate the power of love – that's what keeps me here. It is the most powerful force in the universe. I want to have as much time as possible with you, and I am teaching you about death and your own strengths – these are important lessons. Death is a process, never forget that, not something to be over in a quick moment. Death is like birth – it takes time. Birth is also a painful experience, but we all do it. Death is an adventure into the next life and also a letting-go of those we love in this life. Death can be beautiful if we see it differently.'

As I was relaying Benny's message, I kept hearing *Thrice in a quick moment*. I told Anna I didn't know what it meant, but felt it might be relevant because it was being repeated. Sometimes I receive messages that don't make sense to me but they are relevant to the guardian and over time their true meaning is revealed.

Benny continued, 'Rejoice in my love for you and the power to be able to stay. The time is not yet, my love. *Trust me.* You will know in your heart.'

'I feel so emotional,' Anna shared. 'I am so touched by what he is telling me. I'd always believed Benny was staying on for me and suffering. Will he show me a sign when it's time for him to go?'

'You will know in your heart,' he said, while picturing himself still and barely breathing, his power waning. 'Don't push me over while I am taking pleasure from life. Not yet, my love.'

When animals talk about the time they wish to ascend some can be specific to the last day, the last hour and even the last few minutes. During this communication Benny was clearly stating he didn't want the vet called out then and there, and later we came to learn that he had his own reason for giving such clear direction.

The following day he was struggling to walk and started to eat a slice of meat but gave up on it. Over the course of the day he grew worse and Anna was worried.

She told me later, 'Last night he began to act strangely: he was turning around in circles and wouldn't stop. I started to panic and called the emergency vet for advice.'

The vet advised her to give Benny some medication and it seemed to help. He visibly calmed down. The time was now 3 a.m. and, exhausted, Anna went to bed.

'Then I suddenly woke with a start,' she recalled. 'It was 5 a.m. and I found Benny huddled in a corner outside my daughter's bedroom next to a mosquito plug-in. He was wet and cold. For a moment I thought I'd lost him.'

Anna picked him up, wrapped him in a blanket and placed him on her lap. Stroking him, she said, 'Oh no, Benny, I can't let you go like this, my precious. I love you too much.'

Her heart was aching, but over time she could feel Benny's body warming up.

'I knew then I had to make a decision,' she said. With tears running down her cheeks, she told him, 'Benny, I'm prepared for you to go.'

As soon as she said these words, Benny began to purr and his little paws opened and closed in bliss.

'I had this unexpected feeling of peace in my heart,' Anna said. 'At 9 a.m., still in my arms, he lifted his head and looked at me, asking to get down. His legs were steadier as he walked into the kitchen to have a drink. Totally calm, I picked up the phone and asked the vet to send someone over to put him to sleep later in the afternoon.'

Looking back, it's clear to see that Benny was waiting for Anna to say she was prepared for him to leave her. He wanted her to come to the realization that he couldn't stay with her forever, and above all he wanted her to feel ready to let him go. His will was conquering his body in order for Anna to learn this truth, and when she did, Benny let her know with his paws and purrs he was happy about her new awareness.

The call-out vet was Valentina, someone Anna knew very well. A caring and sensitive woman who had visited Benny at home a number of times, she had commented before, 'Benny's not a cat, he's an angel.'

Anna said, 'I knew the right place for him to go was at home and that Valentina was the right person to look after it. I didn't want him to suffer any longer. Just as Benny had said, *I had a knowing in my heart it was time to let him go.*'

Anna's husband asked her whether she needed anything and she said she'd like him to bring some flowers.

'Mimmo brought five little red roses, which I arranged in the spare room with a perfumed candle and soft classical music in the background. Benny was lying beneath the desk looking comfortable with his front paws tucked under his chest. He looked calm and gave me the impression that he wasn't suffering any more.

Throughout the day I stroked him and said, "Everything's going to be all right, sweetheart," and he purred back at me. I felt he was telling me, "I know." This was one of the hardest moments in my life, but I knew I had to be strong for Benny.'

A bit later it dawned on Anna that she didn't know where she was going to bury Benny's body. Living in an apartment, she didn't have a garden of her own. She called her friend Victoria in a panic and explained her dilemma.

'Anna, it will be a privilege to have Benny in my garden,' Victoria soothed.

The vet was punctual.

'Benny was relaxed as we walked into the room. Valentina gently explained the procedure and reassured me that Benny wouldn't feel a thing. Strangely, I felt strong as I stroked him. Even though my heart was breaking, I was ready.'

The vet sedated Benny before giving him a general anaesthetic. She reassured Anna once more as they waited for his breathing to slow down. Then she administered the final injection. In a split second it was over.

'My immediate feeling was relief – as though a heavy weight had been lifted from my heart. I knew Benny wasn't suffering any more. He looked so peaceful as he lay in the middle of the room on his pastel-grey blanket with the mouse in the corner. I buried my face in his soft little white tummy and kissed him...

I picked two red roses. I laid one next to Benny and placed the other inside the pages of Heart to Heart. *As I said goodbye, the feeling of loss overwhelmed me.*

The following morning as I lay in bed in a state between being asleep and being awake, I felt Benny jump onto my legs. It took me a few seconds to realize that he wasn't with me any more, but I also knew that brief feeling on my legs was him.

I kept myself busy during the day to help ease the pain. As I was walking past the lounge, I saw him. I stopped and looked again, but he was gone. It happened in a split second. He looked so beautiful and I knew then that he was still with me. These moments gave me such comfort.'

A few days later Anna was talking to her daughter-in-law about Benny's passing and recounting how the vet had put him to sleep in three stages: the sedative, the anaesthetic and the last injection, and then in a split second he had gone.

'As I was saying the words, it dawned on me it was what Pea had heard during our communication: *Thrice in a quick moment.* Benny knew what was going to happen.'

A few weeks later, Anna's sister, Juliana, visited. She loved animals too and was interested in Benny's communications and *Heart to Heart*. As she was browsing through the book, she came across the pressed rose Anna had placed there.

'Did you choose this page on purpose?'

'No,' Anna said curiously. 'Why?'

'You've put the rose in the section titled "Street-Cool Sammy".'

Anna told me, 'I had that knowing feeling in my heart that Benny was telling me to focus on looking after my remaining cat, Sammy.'

Later she revealed:

There have been times when I have felt Benny's presence. Especially one night as I was looking out of the window deep in thought and felt Sammy rubbing against my legs. I looked down, then all around, but she wasn't there. I walked into the kitchen and found her fast asleep in her basket. I was astonished when it came to me that it wasn't Sammy rubbing my legs – it was Benny.

Having the communication with Benny totally changed my perspective on life and death. I think most of us are afraid of death. It's the not knowing. But by communicating via Pea, Benny taught me a great lesson: he lessened the fear of death. During the time he gave me, he helped prepare me for his passing and helped me realize it was not the end of him or of our love.

A year later I saw a Spiritualist medium and as I walked into the room he said, "Oh, a little black-and-white cat has come in with you."

Deep in my heart I know that he is always with me, and one day we will be together again. I thank God that I have been blessed with Benny and I will never forget him – my sweetheart, Benny.'

The next chapter continues with my journey with Morgan. It explores who makes the decision to end a life, raises ethical questions about animals being 'put down' and makes the comparison with the ending of a human life.

Chapter 6
Morgan: When is Life Worth Living?

'Life can be beautiful, if only we let it. Good can be seen in the darkest moment. The very darkest moment. If... we allow ourselves to see it.'
MORGAN

After the stroke, Morgan recovered so well that things went back to normal. He was a little less strong, but his zest for running and love of life returned to how they used to be. When he was tired his weakness was visible to those in the know, but most of the time he was just as he'd always been: lovable and pigheaded.

Older dogs often have things going wrong and Morgan was no exception. In February 2010 everything was wonderful until one cold winter's day when he joined in the fun with other dogs careering and skidding across a frozen pond in joyful abandon. He was fine at the time, but later at home I noticed he had begun to shiver. It's easy to forget that paws get cold and older animals can't cope the way young ones do. Morgan was suffering from a mild case of hypothermia.

Hypothermia is very dangerous for dogs. In its severe form it can affect their breathing, circulation, heart and consciousness. Mild and severe forms of hypothermia are treated very differently. If an animal with severe hypothermia is rewarmed incorrectly, it can cause rewarming shock or fatal heart attack. The worst thing you can do for a dog with severe hypothermia is to put them in a warm bath or shower. It's worth researching, because you just never know if you'll need it for your own animal or someone else's.

Just a few days after this incident I was at home alone with Morgan and Texas when out of the blue Morgan began to run up and down the short length of the living room. Then he ran up and down the hall over and again. I didn't understand what was happening, and as his running became more and more manic, I tried holding him to break the cycle, but he struggled and broke free and started running again.

It was out of hours, so the only option was an emergency veterinary appointment. I wondered how I was going to drive Morgan there when he wouldn't stop still even for a moment. Luckily Jenny came to the rescue again and somehow we managed to get Morgan onto the back seat of her car, where I did my best to hold him while she drove. He hated being restrained in the back – he barked and pulled and was desperate to get out. It was the longest 10-minute car journey we'd ever experienced.

Once inside the surgery, I was told to wait there. I looked at the receptionist in amazement. She had failed to comprehend that Morgan couldn't 'wait in reception'. I took him back outside so that he was able to run up and down the high street, which he did, trailing explosive diarrhoea in his wake, while Jenny waited for our names to be called. Nothing I tried would calm him.

Finally our turn came and I walked Morgan into the claustrophobic examination room where the vet failed to greet us and referred to him as a girl. I started to wish I hadn't brought him. She simply told me to go back home and wait for him to calm down. I insisted on some medication to help calm him, because this couldn't go on, he'd been in distress for well over an hour and was completely wiped out. The three of us had another torturous journey back home.

Finally, the medicine started to work and Morgan found some peace. He lay flat out on the floor, utterly drained.

Jo returned and we brought down the spare single mattress to make him comfortable. We closed the blinds to darken the room and when it felt right I played soothing music.

Over the next few days I offered crystal healing. I placed crystal stones in an oval and Morgan walked into the middle and lay down. He stayed like this for over half an hour and drifted off to sleep, soaking up the subtle energetic vibrations of the different rocks. As with his day-to-day care, I offered the crystal healing intuitively, relying on what I felt was good for him. It took several days before he showed signs of recovery.

In a way this seizure could have been scarier than his stroke, because Morgan was in greater visible physical distress and he wasn't communicating what he felt or wanted; he was so overwhelmed by his condition it was as though he was somewhere else completely. But this time I felt more in control. We'd been in crisis before and I knew this wasn't the end. Morgan had said we'd have two more years together and I trusted him. I was strong and calm and could easily envision his recovery.

In the same month as the seizure Morgan bravely sat for photographs for the front cover of the *Daily Mail* magazine. There was a possibility we'd be chosen for the front cover to accompany their feature on *Heart to Heart*. Morgan understood why I was asking him to pose (not his thing) and although very tired and still recovering, he sat quietly, moved with me to new positions and looked towards the camera on cue as Jenny dangled a treat in the air. Six hours later the team finally left. Morgan had never complained, he had never tried to leave; he had simply been tolerant and incredibly patient. I know he gave so much of himself for me that day. The photo of us on the front cover of this book was taken about four hours in. It still makes me emotional years later to remember how generous he was in service to me, and ultimately to human awakening.

Gradually over the next few months Morgan regained his strength and returned to his joyful self, pottering or running across commons and taking a huge interest in everything food-related. In May 2010 he went lame on a front leg and was diagnosed with a trapped nerve, but acupuncture and homoeopathy made a real difference and he gradually made a full recovery. During this time he taught me so much about patience, persistence and positivity.

'I Came Here for a Purpose'

In November 2010 Morgan was featured in an MA final exhibition at the London College of Communication. The student photographer, Zhao Yiyi, called her work 'I Came Here for a Purpose'. The exhibition reflected human–animal communication and included some of Morgan's messages:

> Q: 'Who are you? What is your purpose?'
> A: 'My name has always been Love. This is who I am.'
> Q: 'What is your message to the world?'
> A: 'Life can be beautiful, if only we let it. Good can be seen in the darkest moment.' The very darkest moment. If... we allow ourselves to see it.'
> Q: 'What is your purpose for the world?'
> A: 'My purpose is to spread Love. It always has been.'
> Q: Is there anything else you'd like to tell people?'
> A: 'Life is beautiful.'
> Q: 'Anything further?'
> A: 'I am happy and grateful.'

When I asked Texas for a comment, he wasn't in the mood, so under duress he replied very quickly, 'All ginger cats are beautiful. We are the Master Species. Honour our beautiful presence in your life.' Then he finished with, 'Let me sleep now.'

A book was created for the project and there was my handwritten message at the end:

> *'Morgan has told me we are connected all the time and what affects one will affect another, across any distance. His message and the message the other animals give is to respect and love all sentient beings.'*

As Happy and Comfortable as Possible

The following months continued as normal – no further strokes or seizures, just lots of happy times and delicious food. Morgan taught at some workshops and delighted in sharing interspecies communication with the students. As time passed, however, he began to do what older sentient beings do: run less, walk more and tire more easily.

17 April 2011

As he's a rescue, we don't know Morgan's exact birthday, but we will celebrate it today. He requests the presence of his human friends, his golden retriever pal and, most importantly, 'human cake'. He rises to the occasion and is always in the middle of the action. He eats his birthday cake, a Victoria sponge, with great gusto, returns for a second slice and grins from ear to ear, his eyes sparkling. Once everyone has gone he zonks out, exhausted but immensely content.

A year after his seizure Morgan was weaker and not always aware of what he was doing. It had been two years since his stroke and prediction, and I was aware we were on borrowed time. Hearteningly, those two years had been fulfilled years of happiness.

Morgan had a wart to the side of his spine which had been there for a few years. It didn't bother him and he wasn't in pain, but over time it had grown more pronounced. Jo and I called it a wart, but deep down we knew it was some kind of tumour. At roughly 17 years old and vet-phobic, Morgan was clear he didn't want any invasive medical interaction and would rather focus on quality of life rather than quantity. We agreed and decided against anything exploratory. Maybe it was cancerous, maybe it wasn't. Even if a needle aspiration came back positive, we'd decided we weren't going down the line of chemotherapy or other cancer treatments. Instead we both agreed with Morgan's wish and focused on the here and now.

Everything revolved around making Morgan as happy and comfortable as possible.

21 May: 'How Do You Feel?'

Today has become a continuation of last night. Morgan is sleeping for short stints but much of the time he is restless. Pacing. Walking round in circles until I intervene and place him back in his bed.

I feel the pacing is due to two conditions, senility being one of them. Over the past year Morgan has had moments of fazing out and freezing, then wondering what he was doing. He has also communicated to me that he's had two mini-strokes. He's gradually lost the use of his left side and really can't feel much of his left hind foot at all. He finds this most frustrating, but despite these physical setbacks, on a telepathic level he is still sharp.

I know it's very hard seeing our animals struggle when they are older and sick. We want to protect them and can't bear the thought of them suffering. This is why it's helpful to ask them directly how they feel rather than presuming life's becoming too much.

I ask Morgan, 'How do you feel?'

'I feel content. That's all you need to know.'

I guess this is truly what it boils down to. Is your animal friend still content? If Morgan is content, he'll want to keep going despite the setbacks and frustrations. It's the desire that's important, the desire to keep going, to keep engaging with life.

After supper I lift him up onto the sofa next to me, having already covered it in blankets and a fleece to make it 'wart-proof'. The growth has grown and split and often oozes pus. Sometimes he knocks it and it bleeds over his white hair. I guess I'm used to the smell now, having lived with it so long, but I imagine my friends find it pretty unpleasant. They are polite and don't comment, but we don't encourage visitors now. It's just us, the family, and we like it like this.

22 May

The radio is on and a Bob Marley track connects with me like a direct message from Morgan. He's singing that there's no need to worry because everything's going to be all right.

After 15 minutes of strokes, healing and gratitude, from me to him, Morgan decides it is his bedtime. The routine is always the same. Give him his bedtime snack (fresh chicken). Carry his bed upstairs. Prepare the room: blinds closed, water bowl full, overhead light off, sidelight on low, rugs in place protecting the carpet, spare bedding for a middle of the night bed-change and a check on the temperature – not too hot but not chilly either. By the time I've done all that, Morgan has finished his chicken and is waiting at the bottom of the stairs for his ride. I carry him up.

I remember a time when he refused to be picked up and held. He spent years refusing to have anyone fuss over him, barely tolerating Jo or me giving him a swift lift up into the back of the car.

Even now he wants to get down as soon as possible and prefers to wobble the remaining length of the landing rather than be carried all the way to the bedroom. After a couple of staggering-drunk laps of the room he allows me to settle him into his bed and happily has me sit with him for a while.

After leaving him alone for five minutes, I always go back to check he is still settled. If he's turned himself round and curled up facing the window then I know that's him off to sleep – for however long that will be. This evening at the five-minute check I find he's had a disagreement with his water bowl. He is in a heap on the floor and his legs are soaking wet. The water bowl has won. I towel-dry his legs and lift him back into bed. Before I've even left the room he has started drifting off. The water fight has tired him out.

Caring is all part of the responsibility and unconditional love that guardians have for their animal companions. One of our roles as guardians is to honour their dying process by providing comfort, support and reassurance.

'Am I Keeping You Here?'

When our animals are very sick or heading towards the end of their life, our friends can be super-supportive. They can also say all the wrong things. Sometimes there's pressure from well-meaning friends to 'let them go'. People will say 'you are keeping them here against their will' or 'they are staying just for you'. In these moments, trust your own intuition. Trust what your animal is communicating to you.

23 May

I look across to Morgan and wait to see if he'll comment on the idea that I am keeping him here against his will or he is staying just for me.

'What rubbish!' he says.

Morgan is loving and generous, but he's also strong-minded, and I know in my heart he'll go when he is ready and only then.

'I'll Keep Going and Caring for You'

Some people find it very hard to see dying through to the end. Before animal communication I couldn't even talk about death because I felt it was the end, finite, a blackness of non-existence. It was a scary thought. The animals I've communicated with have taught me to view it differently. I now see death as a changing point for the soul. It's a time when a sick, injured, worn-out or damaged body is left behind and there is the opportunity for the soul to renew itself for a new experience, whether that is by reincarnating into a new physical form or by remaining in an energetic soul form.

28 May: Caring Can Be Hard Work

It has been a terrible day; Morgan has hardly settled, he has fallen down a lot and he can't drink by himself. I am now syringing water into his mouth, although he's reluctant to take it. He is, however, eating lots of chicken and white fish, which is a good sign.

He finally settles about 7.30 p.m. At last some rest.

It's 9 p.m. now and he is trying to climb out of bed, but without full control of his legs he just keeps travelling to his right and then collapsing. I cross the living room to help him.

A little later he is eating some fish in the kitchen but struggling to stand. I lift him back up and then realize his wart is bleeding over my clothes. Blood is also running down Morgan's leg hair, covering his white paw with red goo. The bleed goes on for what feels like forever as I try to stop it and steady him with my legs at the same time. Why steady him? Because, completely unfazed, he is continuing to demolish the bowl of coley.

There is another tiny hiccup: a toilet indiscretion. I won't say more – you know what I mean. Before his senility began he was always a very clean dog. But bodily functions are all part and parcel of caring for an elderly sentient being, human or non-human.

Tonight I ask him again, 'Are you content?'

He replies, 'Not as much.'

Tomorrow I need to repeat the question. He may still want to eat, but it's clear his sparkle is dulling now.

As I take him up to bed I say to him, 'I'll keep going and caring for you for as long as you want to keep going.'

And that is my promise to him. But I admit it is hard. I am so tired now. For months I've been up every night numerous times and his daytime care is a big commitment on top of my full-time practice completing client communications and teaching workshops.

29 May: A Bad Sign

I tell Jo, 'Morgan's energy is really small today. It's very low.'

He isn't drinking and is very unhappy whenever I try to syringe water into his mouth. He just doesn't want it.

Sometimes when you're so close to an animal it's good to ask for external help. Today is that day; I want to double-check how Morgan is doing and, without giving any information, I ask friends to communicate with him. One phones me back straightaway and says his energy is very small, which is what I'm feeling, and then goes on to say he's getting ready to ascend. However, while we are still on the phone Morgan lifts his head and turns to look at me.

'I'm not letting go,' he tells me. Then adds, 'Warm water.'

It's now 3:44 p.m., and he's accepted six syringes of warm water. His wart has been bleeding again and his snoozes only last for 20 minutes before he's circling again. However, after the last three syringes of water and a further bleed, he's now draped in his bed with a glint in his eye and a bit of a cheeky smile on his face. He amazes me by how quickly he can begin to recover.

Warm water – why didn't I think of that?

It has been a difficult day, but I hold on to what Morgan has told me: 'I'm not letting go.'

Besides emotional support, everything else becomes practicality: syringing, cleaning and lifting.

I recognize that the agony I feel at losing Morgan comes when I lose touch with the truth that his beautiful spirit – his soul – will continue and is simply stepping out of his old and aged body. I remind myself of a truth: separation is an illusion. 'We are all connected, all of the time, across any distance.'

30 May: 'I Want Some More'

This morning Morgan manages a bowl of white fish with a little water, followed by some chicken. Then he states, 'I want some more,' and eats another two bowls of chicken.

Today I get out of the house to restore my emotional strength and to gain some perspective, doing something beautifully mundane: the weekly shop. It may not be your idea of time out, but anything that provides a break from caring for a sick or elderly animal will be beneficial – it gives perspective and the heart some important restorative time.

I come back with one of Morgan's old favourites: a custard tart. After an initial sniff, he takes a piece and it's gone in a flash. I offer him another piece and there's no hesitation. Texas even saunters over and asks for a piece. I suggest Morgan has the rest in his bowl and he's up on his feet following me up the step and out to the breakfast room. Morgan of the old days suddenly takes over: he wolfs down the custard tart and returns to the bowl a couple of times to make sure it's all gone. He amazes me by standing over his bowl with his legs straight and his back flat – all due to the magical properties of a custard tart!

Strive to Be Happy

I know it won't be long before Morgan becomes the Light that he is. I ask him, 'Is there anything you'd like to say?'

'Life is about happiness. To strive to be happy. Happiness is in being rather than doing.'

'But as humans we have to work to earn money to pay our bills,' I counter him.

'That's all very well, but you can do it mindfully. Many rush around without a thought of what they are doing. They become robotic – living for another moment, rather than the one they're in. That's all I mean.'

'Can we talk about death?' I ask.

'Yes, please,' he replies.

There is a moment's silence between us.

Then Morgan communicates, 'Death is where life begins again. It is not the end, as is perceived. It is a changing of the guard, a changing of role. The energy becomes pure. It becomes its purest form again – back to where it started.'

'Do you fear death?'

'Of course not.'

'Do you fear anything?'

'Being without you.'

My strength dissolves.

'Morgan, what I feel is that we have a strong soul connection. I feel we are both finding it hard to let go of our attachment. Yet I know we are now. I feel you drifting away from me.'

Morgan explains, 'When you're ready for death, you're so worn out that your energy begins to spread. Your physical body moves down to the ground and the Earth connection and your spirit learns to separate. Yes, learns to separate. Because, although I have done this process many times, on a soul level I forget and have to learn it all over again. It sometimes feels familiar, like a comforting robe, and at other times it feels as though I am drifting in deep water all alone. Death is a process both for those left behind and for those going through it. It is a learning process of letting go for all. While I am ready to let go of this body, I am not ready yet to let go of my pleasure in food and of the love you give me. These earthly pleasures still buoy my heart and keep me from sinking further.'

31 May: 'When Is All Life Equal?

Today has been tricky. There have been two visitors: some cleaning help we have at the moment who just says 'Oh my God' every time she sees Morgan, and a friend who thinks it's easier to make the decision for an animal.

But is it really what the animal wants?

What's not so easy is seeing Morgan have bright-yellow diarrhoea, witnessing his wart bleed, being unable to stop it, and having to do the endless day and night bedding changes. Today I realize quite acutely that it takes strength to keep the care going and to honour the wishes of your animal.

I don't see why this is any different from caring for an elderly relative at the end of their life. Why, when it comes to animals, is it socially taboo or not convenient? Who makes the decision to end a life – to put an animal to sleep? Are the animals allowed to be involved in their own end-of-life decision?

If we envision for a moment that all life is equal, why would we approach the end of a non-human animal life differently from that of a human animal life? Would we 'put down' a person showing signs of old age or arthritis? In the same vein; would we discard or destroy humans showing signs of aggression or proving too costly to keep? When is all life equal?

Morgan has taught me that his opinion matters. That he knows his body well and also, maybe more importantly, the strength of his will. He is able to explain what he is feeling and when something is important and when it is not. Imagine a world where all companion animals are respectfully given the opportunity to share their feelings and their wishes for the end of their life. How would that look?

Preparations

By this time I had started to make preparations. I had begun to look into arrangements for cremation. I am not against burial, but Morgan had requested his ashes be released. I wanted to be prepared and to avoid a last-minute panic to locate an ethical crematorium which put the animal's dignity first and also showed compassion towards the guardians. How to find such a place?

As luck would have it, a client told me about Dignity, a pet crematorium in Hampshire, where she had taken her own dog. It just so happened that Jo, Morgan and I were going to be driving virtually past the door, so we organized a visit to check it out.

We'd been on a cottage holiday near Glastonbury, blankets, towels, wart 'n' all. Morgan had a great time pottering around the field behind us and enjoying the smells of other animals. He even walked up Glastonbury Tor. One morning he took us by complete surprise when from nowhere he began to run ecstatically, wearing the biggest grin and seemingly in complete control of his legs. Joy erupted from him. There was life in our old dog yet.

Together we took a tour of the Dignity grounds. Far from feeling miserable, it actually seemed like a good time to be checking out such a place. It felt right to Jo and me, but we wanted Morgan's opinion. Why shouldn't he have a say? He replied, 'Yes, this one,' and so it was decided. That was the crematorium agreed.

We also considered the option of euthanasia. I would have preferred Morgan to have an unassisted passing, but I knew this was not always possible. I also recognized that 'natural' deaths were not always peaceful.

I believe there is nothing wrong with euthanasia under the right circumstances, when it is the right time for the animal. The word itself is from the Greek, meaning 'good death'. The British House of Lords Select Committee on Medical Ethics defines euthanasia as a 'deliberate intervention undertaken with the express intention of ending a life, to relieve intractable suffering'. In the Netherlands, euthanasia is understood as 'termination of life by a doctor at the request of the patient'. Francis Bacon first used the word in a medical context back in the seventeenth century to refer to an easy, painless, happy death during which it was a 'physician's responsibility to alleviate the "physical sufferings" of the body'. The main points here are *to relieve intractable suffering* and *at the request of the patient*, which in this respect is the animal.

There are many ethical questions over euthanasia, mainly built upon personal religious beliefs. This is how I choose to look at it: will euthanasia ease suffering? Is the timing correct for the animal and nothing to do with convenience or financial cost? Is it for the best interests of the animal on the receiving end? And has the animal communicated their desire to transition with assisted help? They can do this through telepathic communication and also through a look or body language. Often a guardian will *just know*.

I also believe, where there is time, it helps to prepare the soul for transition before death by euthanasia. The animal's soul can be honoured with a small ceremony, a few kind words, candles, music, poems or whatever comes to mind that shows respect and celebrates the animal's life. I know that sadly not everyone can do this. But if you have lost an animal through sudden death or accident, you can still hold the ceremony afterwards, because my belief is that it is never too late to honour an animal's soul essence.

My biggest concern is how we view the care of non-human animals in comparison to human animals. Would we euthanize our granny because of the cost of keeping her in a care home? Would we consider the time and energy it takes to look after a sick parent and decide against it because it's going to encroach on our lifestyle or we've got a holiday booked? If our child loses a limb, would we put them down because a one-legged child is inconvenient, unattractive or no longer fits requirements? I think all of our decisions around the care of animals and how best to ease their suffering needs to be done with heartfelt consciousness and we may need to answer uncomfortable questions like 'Am I treating this animal with the same care and consideration that I would show to a human being?'

I chose to support Morgan 24/7 because I loved him and because he loved life and he wanted more of it. As an equal and sentient being under my care, this was the least he deserved from me.

We may not think that euthanasia, burial or cremation are important to animals, but so many animals do have views on these things. I can't paint all animals with the same brush, because each animal is an individual; some care more than others and some want to do what's most comforting for their guardian.

You may prefer not to look into practical considerations ahead of time, and that's OK – it's your decision. All I can impart is that when the time came to release Morgan, practicalities were the last thing I wanted to engage with. I wanted all of my attention to be focused on him.

In the next chapter you'll read about Greecia, a cat who answers the questions 'Do you want to pass over?' and 'Would you like an assisted death or prefer to go by yourself?'

Chapter 7
Greek Goddess Greecia

❦

'No one wants to be in pain, darling.'
GREECIA

Like many cats, Greecia knew her own mind. She was able to give startling details of what she wanted at the end of her life and a precise request for her ashes. She was aware of how sick she was and how far she could push herself before she needed to let go, and she was clear on how she wanted that to happen.

Printing off Greecia's photo, I was struck by the stern, superior face of a tabby and white cat with a sly grin. Yes, a sly grin. I'd never met anyone quite like Greecia. She had rivers of saddle-brown running through her thick jet-black fur and a white muzzle, chest and legs. In Greek mythology black was the colour of the underworld. It was also one of the most important colours used by Greek artists, and with Greecia it had been used to beautiful effect. Greecia had an intensity about her too. Her green eyes showed there were clear boundaries which were not to be crossed. She was almost warrior-like.

Greecia, otherwise known as Gree, Gree Gree, Greecia Gherkin and the Gree Cat, was called Greecia because Jean felt she was very beautiful and deserved a beautiful name. Originally her name was pronounced *Greethia*, but it became Greecia very soon after.

A friend had asked Jean if she wanted to take on a kitten as her farmer friend had too many and needed to find them homes. When she visited, there were three kittens in the farm kitchen. She felt great love for Greecia as soon as she laid eyes on her and took her home straightaway.

It came as no surprise when I connected with Greecia's energy that I sensed a strong character who didn't like to be messed with. Greecia was feisty. She showed me she was sleeping a lot but trying to eat tiny pieces of fresh chicken. I felt her heart racing and her frailty. I could sense she had lost weight and was thin and weak now. She explained that she loved biscuits but had some problem with her teeth. She showed an image of sleeping close to a radiator and then I sensed problems with her kidneys – the energy of this resonated to me like renal failure.

I must have been communicating with enough respect because Greecia then dropped her barriers and allowed me to sense that she was very sweet with Jean, rubbing round her legs at feeding time and coming when called. Underneath the armoured exterior was a soft, sweet cat with a heart of gold. Greecia was loyal and I felt she adored her guardian.

I e-mailed these first impressions and Jean replied:

> *'Greecia is looking skinny and not eating very much.*
> *She has always had trouble with her teeth; it costs me a*
> *fortune in vet bills every year and quite a few teeth have*
> *been removed. My partner, Gus, and I took her to the vet*
> *to be checked over because I was worried she had kidney*
> *problems. I used to look after my mum's cat, Tiddly*
> *(who was a rather large ginger tom), and he had kidney*
> *problems. The vet took Greecia's bloods but was not too*

*hopeful about the prognosis. It has been confirmed she
does have kidney failure. She also has hyperthyroidism;
her heart is racing and she's very low in potassium. I feel
devastated. I have experienced some very troubled times
and Greecia has always been my one constant. She rubs
her face all over mine and jumps on my lap whenever I sit
down. I simply adore her. We are a team, Gree and I. She
is my world.'*

Jean had only seen the soft, sweet side of Greecia and had never considered that she was strong and feisty. This occasionally happens when a guardian is only exposed to one side of their companion's character. Greecia had never needed to let Jean know she was overstepping boundaries because Jean had never crossed them.

'My mum was a great animal lover and stray cats often found their way to us,' Jean told me. 'I was brought up to understand that animals were beings with their own feelings, likes and dislikes, and that I should be respectful of their boundaries.'

She expressed a necessity to hear from Greecia as soon as possible, so we arranged a telephone appointment for the next available space.

Jean started by asking about the potassium she was giving Greecia: 'She hates being given the tablets and it breaks my heart each time we have to force them down, but they seem to enable her to eat just a little bit. I've been very torn deciding what's best for her.'

'Greecia says they help her stomach,' I explained.

We then reached the vital questions: 'Is it time for her to pass over and is she ready to go?'

Greecia answered, 'No, not yet. Nearly, though. A few more days, please.'

I gently explained to Jean that I'd communicated with Greecia two days prior to this telephone appointment, which suggested 'a few more days' was very close. Jean had instinctively felt the same and she'd already booked a veterinary appointment for the following morning.

'I want her to know how important she has been in my life and how much I have appreciated her unconditional love,' she managed to say before sobbing uncontrollably.

I gave Jean the time and understanding she needed as her loss rose to the surface. She was already experiencing what is known as pre-grief – real grief in the anticipation of loss.

I listened to Greecia's reply, then gently repeated it: 'Greecia loves and adores you and this will never end. She wants you to know this and to understand you have been her number one and very special in her life too. She says she has always, *always*, enjoyed your company.'

'I can't believe I am going to be without my Gree after 18 years together,' Jean said. 'I know the pain that is coming and it is almost too much to bear. Greecia and I have a very special bond and I know that her connection to me is as strong as mine to her. Please tell her I'm sorry that I'm having to give her tablets and food when she doesn't want them, but I'm trying to do my best with the knowledge I have. It is heartbreaking seeing her so thin and tired. She approaches the food bowl and then she just can't eat anything. It is torturous to watch and we are trying everything to whet her appetite. I guess a bit of me thinks if I can just tempt her to eat she will be stronger and we will have some more time together. Is there anything she would like to eat?'

'Nothing at all, really. Every time I eat I feel sick,' Greecia responded.

Animals sometimes stop eating and refuse medication when they wish to begin the process of letting go of their body. Not all, though – some eat up to the very last moment. Dogs, especially, like to get in a last meal before they pass. It is also worth remembering that some animals go off their food when they are in pain, and with an appropriate level of pain-relief their appetite returns.

Greecia then gave a series of images. 'She's picturing being at home on a blue cushion and up off the ground. I believe she's showing how she'd like to pass over,' I said.

Greecia continued by showing herself going to sleep peacefully at home, assisted by a woman with dark bob-like hair.

Jean confirmed:

'I'd planned on placing my navy-blue cushion on my lap for her to lie on when she was assisted over. So that's just how I'd planned it. With one exception – I was going to take her into the surgery, but I'll change that now I know her wishes.

The reason this is important to me is because of my mum and her cat, Tiddly. In her final hours I promised my mum I would take care of Tiddly and he lived with me for five healthy years before taking a turn for the worse with kidney problems. The vet broke the news that he was in terrible pain and would have to be put to sleep. I had to leave him overnight at the surgery. It happened to be bonfire night and I knew Tiddly hated fireworks. I lay in bed listening to them going off, knowing he was in a pen and probably terrified. I didn't sleep.

The next morning I went to where he was in a cage with a catheter and drip attached. He mewed then tried to stand and crawl into my arms. I was shocked. The vet was amazed and said it was the most movement Tiddly had made since I'd taken him in.

I said my goodbyes and told Tiddly what a good friend he had been, then the vet came to put him to sleep. It was the most terrible thing. Tiddly yelped as the solution was injected into him. He looked distressed and then he was gone. Bubbles started to come from his nose. I knew he had been in pain and I hadn't wanted to move him, but I was wracked with guilt that I hadn't asked for the tubes to be removed so I could hold him on my lap. He had been my faithful friend, a joy in my life, and I had let him down when he needed me. I still carry this with me years later. This is why Greecia's passing has to be planned and she has to know that I am still there with her on her last journey.'

We continued with the communication and Jean's message for Greecia: 'Please tell her I'm sorry that I've made some wrong decisions over the years.'

Many caring guardians wish to say this to their animals and I always feel it's worth doing. Animals are very forgiving, but do often like an apology. When I asked Morgan why, he told me, 'Because it helps heal the guardian's heart.'

Greecia's reply to Jean was simple: 'There is nothing to forgive or worry about. I love you.'

'Let her know I'm sorry her space was invaded by the ginger moggy, but I felt I had to look after him.'

'I would have preferred him not to be there. The space alone. You alone. To myself. I have tolerated him,' she said bluntly but without malice.

'Oh, she has,' said Jean. 'She has tolerated him. Tiddly was a very big character and he took up space in my heart that had previously been Greecia's. She wasn't amused by his arrival and would wave her paw angrily at him as he walked past, usually oblivious. I knew she was unhappy about it and I'm sorry. What can I do to help her and make her happy?'

The Greek goddess warrior answered, 'Cuddle me a lot. Soft, smooth gentle strokes.' She went on to picture kisses on her head with a feeling of happiness.

'Greecia looks too frail for cuddles and chin "chugglings", so I have taken to kissing her very gently on the head each time I pass and telling her I love her,' Jean told me. Then she checked, 'Does she want an assisted death?'

Greecia responded gently, 'Yes. No one wants to be in pain, darling. But not yet.'

Animals will often reply 'Not yet' when they are telling their guardian *not immediately*.

'I had thought to scatter Greecia's ashes with my mum's and Tiddly's,' Jean continued. 'It'll feel as though she'll be going into my mother's arms, but I have misgivings, as the two cats didn't get along. Where would Greecia like to be scattered? Shall I scatter her with Tiddly?'

'No, not with him,' Greecia snapped.

She finished the communication with an image of a narrow-trunked tree with leaves on the branches. Peculiarly, the branches didn't begin by going out horizontally then angling up, but extended upwards like the ribs of an upside-down umbrella. I had a feeling it was a fruit tree, maybe a pear.

Greecia showed the tree on the left side of a garden and also added, 'To the left.' She showed herself sleeping to the right of the tree and ended the communication with 'Don't worry, dear.'

That night Jean slept downstairs on an airbed in the lounge so she could be close to Greecia during her last night.

The next morning her regular vet arrived, along with a female assistant with the brown bob-like hair that Greecia had described.

Jean sat in a chair in front of the French doors overlooking the garden with Greecia positioned on the blue cushion on her lap.

'Greecia made a move to jump from my lap and the assistant held her gently but firmly. At this point she just seemed to relax as if she knew it was time.'

From their seated position both Jean and Greecia were able to look out into the garden as Greecia passed over, gently letting go in the manner she'd requested. Jean wrote and told me what had happened:

'After she'd passed her body rose and a sigh came out. Startled, I looked at the vet. She told me that this happened sometimes, but Greecia was gone already. She took two clippings of her fur, so my niece and I could keep a part of her.

We placed Gree in a box. She was still on the cushion and curled up as though she was asleep. My partner and I held each other and sobbed. We took turns to stroke her for one last time and tell her how much she was loved. I held the box on my lap like precious cargo as my partner drove us out to a countryside pet crematorium.

I have to admit the pet crematorium was chosen on price, as I'm currently unemployed. It wasn't until my partner and I were driving down the winding country lanes that I realized we were in the countryside where I'd first chosen Greecia from the farm litter. I remarked to my partner, "It feels a bit like taking her home."

A few weeks later we went to my sister's home to scatter her ashes under the tree. Greecia had stayed with my sister when I'd gone back to London to study at university. She'd loved rubbing around her ankles while she hung the washing out, lazing in the sun in the garden and being groomed by my nephew and niece.

It was a sunny day. Every member of my family and Greecia's extended family scattered some of her ashes and we stood in silence remembering how she was the most brilliant cat.

One morning a few weeks after her passing, I know this might sound strange, but Greecia was taking up the whole of the inside of my head. I could picture her – she was looking young and vibrant. She was just sitting up looking at me. I hadn't been dreaming of her and I know I was definitely awake when this happened. I'm sure she was making her presence felt.

One month after Greecia had passed I asked her to send me a whisker. I needed a sign to know she was all right. Later I was photographing items on the blank background of the floor to sell on Ebay and was reaching down to replace one ready for the next photo when I was struck by the sight of a long white whisker on the floor. I was delighted. I knew it couldn't have been Tiddly's, as he'd passed away while I was still living in London. The room I was in had been vacuumed a number of times since Greecia had died. I felt that this was the sign I'd been asking for and Greecia was saying hello.'

Jean found the communication with Greecia had given her peace of mind.

'I know when my previous cat was put to sleep the guilt was terrible and I was in pieces for months. This time Greecia passed peacefully with no resistance. I felt I had fully honoured her wishes and this was a great comfort.

I wouldn't have asked for a home visit if Greecia hadn't requested it. The description she gave of the tree was also important. Initially I thought it was in my garden, but when I texted my sister, she sent me a photo message which exactly fitted the description Gree had given. The tree was on the left side of her garden and it even leaned to the left.

*It was a plum tree with a narrow trunk and branches like
upside-down umbrella ribs, just as she'd said. Greecia
had loved the sun and my sister's company, so we fulfilled
her final request and scattered her ashes there. Whenever
I stay at my sister's I'm in a bedroom that overlooks the
garden and I often stand gazing out at the tree saying a
few words to my Greecia.*

*I miss her terribly, but I don't have the all-encompassing
guilt that I had with Tiddly. The only problem now is
that I am having terrible issues with whether I should
be veggie again. I was vegetarian for 20 years. Animal
communication certainly throws up things to think about.*

*My communication has also changed my view of the
pet/"owner" relationship. It is very clear that Greecia was
the evolved being and I've been blessed to have her living
alongside me. I am now aware I never "owned" her at all.'*

In her communication Greecia was able to convey that she knew
she was very ill and when and how she wanted to transition. She
was also able to communicate the finer details of her preferred
place of rest. By giving her an opportunity to communicate her
wishes, Jean had been able to release herself from confusion and
the guilt that accompanies it. Each had been able to offer the
other comfort at this significant time and experience peace in the
process of death.

The next chapter continues with Morgan and the strength he
exhibits as he strives to experience the one thing he wants above
all: more life. It also reveals my own mental struggle to go against
others and to listen to my intuition and what Morgan is asking
of me.

Chapter 8
Morgan: 'I Want More Life'

'I am brave. There is nothing to fear.'
MORGAN

2 June 2011

Hallelujah! Morgan is now back on form. His walks mainly involve tootling around his garden, but sometimes he wants to go to his special woods or up and down the street. Occasionally Jo and I drive him to his favourite common and take a little picnic to a quiet spot. We know he likes being there, because joy bursts from his body and his eyes sparkle.

He says, 'I feel peaceful.'

Texas is very undemanding while Morgan needs a lot of one-to-one help. Special Texas-time is at night, when he receives lots of strokes and love and in return purrs up by my face and helps me drift off to sleep. I know he understands and is offering support.

'Do I Look Bovvered?'

There are hiccups. I put down Morgan's dinner and check he is able to hold himself and eat unassisted. Then I go to run some water into a saucepan. A minute or so later I check back and find him lying on his right side against the skirting board with his head stuck sideways in his food bowl. He is struggling to get purchase on the carpet by pushing his head down into the bowl, but he is getting nowhere very fast.

For a few seconds I feel devastated for him as I rush over to help him back to his feet. Yet it isn't heartbreaking for long, because as soon as Morgan is upright he sits down, puts his face back into his bowl and resumes eating with so much gusto it's as though nothing has happened.

'Look at the truth,' he tells me, while continuing to chomp.

'The truth is you're not bothered by what just happened, are you?' I say, sitting on the floor.

'Do I look bothered?' he says, and I immediately think of the comedian Catherine Tate and her schoolkid character Lauren. 'Bovvered? Do I look bovvered? Am I bovvered?' While Morgan finishes his chicken I sit behind him laughing.

3 June: 'Who is Suffering?'

Just when things have levelled out, along comes another challenging day. The first wart bleed is mid-afternoon. Our dark red carpet has a small pool of the dark glossy liquid.

The second bleed is soon after. I'm sweeping out the boot of my car in preparation for putting in workshop crates. I've left the front door open but the gate shut so Morgan can wander out safely for fresh air and a change of scene. Halfway through cleaning out the boot, I look over the gate to check on him and see spots of blood leading into the house. He is nowhere to be seen.

Following the trail into the hall, I discover red pawprints in arty design against the starkness of the black and white tessellated tiles. Morgan is lying down in the hall on the fawn carpet off-cuts, blood oozing down his side and causing a dark red stain at his elbow, which in turn is dripping and turning his white paw red.

Trying to stop the bleed, I find my palms turning solid red, along with the fawn carpet. Imagine my surprise when I look up from my bloodied hands and see Morgan smiling at me.

'It was an accident,' he says, with a glint in his eyes. Then he says again, 'Look at the truth.'

I take a deep breath and exhale slowly. I can see with clarity that Morgan isn't distressed in the slightest.

'I know, sweetheart,' I reply, acknowledging the real truth in front of me.

Looking at the Truth

So, does the heartache come when we don't look at the clear picture? Is the truth that this animal finds their physical limitations and weakness frustrating but is still enjoying their life? Are we the ones making a song and dance over the situation? Maybe we're drawing attention to ourselves without conscious awareness. The 'poor me' scenario: *'Look what I'm going through!'*

It is useful to keep asking ourselves questions. Am I holding them here when they'd rather transition and leave their body? Are they taking pleasure in moments throughout the day? Do they still have a sense of humour and a glint in their eyes? Are they showing signs that they want to keep on living?

If possible, ask *them*. How do you feel emotionally? Physically? Do you need some intervention – help from a vet, a chiropractor, an acupuncturist, a homoeopath or some other practitioner?

Another truth to bear in mind: there will be good days and bad days.

6 June: All is Well

Monday morning at the welcome later time of 6:30 a.m., Morgan lets me know it's time to be carried downstairs for the usual morning routine. After relieving himself in the garden, he gobbles down his breakfast and licks the bowl clean. He has sparkly, sharp eyes and I feel his happiness. The rest of the day is peaceful. All is well.

16 June: Two Days Apart

Morgan has had two terrible days. The first was on Sunday when I was away all day teaching a Sacred Cow animal communication workshop in collaboration with a herd of 30 cows and Tom, an intuitive farmer on a biodynamic farm in West Sussex. Morgan was totally restless and wouldn't settle.

The following day I was resting at home with him and he was peaceful, then there was a moment when I thought he would slip away. His third eyelid was elevated, making his eyes look as though they were rolling into the back of his head, and his energy was very, very flat. I texted Jo to get home quick. Luckily she was close by and five minutes later she walked through the door to find me sitting on the living-room floor next to Morgan with tears gently rolling down my face and my hand on his chest.

Morgan, of course, recovered. It isn't his time just yet.

What I have come to understand about that moment is that his soul was having time out of his physical form. For a short while he was learning to be without a body – to be pure spirit. I believe when the soul has time to do this, when there isn't a sudden death of form, the soul travels between body and pure spirit to experience what it will be like when it has left the body behind. It's preparation for complete separation from physical form.

On Tuesday, I was out all day at a zoo after an invitation to help a keeper with a wolf. Morgan's wart was bleeding repeatedly and this was troubling for Jo. When I got home Morgan was drained of energy but otherwise all right, while Jo was quite unhappy.

It was the culmination of a difficult few days, because Jo and I disagreed on how Morgan was doing. Jo is often away with work and when she's at home she sees him struggling and finding life hard. I am home most of the time and I see a dog who is trying to hang on to life for as long as possible. I witness the rollercoaster of bad days and good days.

Do Animals Hang on for Us? Or Themselves?

Many people feel that if an animal is struggling they are hanging on because their guardian is keeping them here. This is true in some circumstances. It's beneficial to let our animals know they have our consent to leave, to reassure them that we will be OK and they don't need to worry about us any more. It's also kind to acknowledge they must do what they need to do.

Why do people believe an animal is only staying for the guardian? Why can't animals be staying for their own accord? Why do we presume everything revolves around us? Can't the animals make a decision? Can't they make the most important decision of their life – when *they* want to die? Do humans have to control everything?

Above all else we need to remember that individual animals and guardians create individual situations. We can listen to other people's point of view, but we don't necessarily have to agree. We should listen to the inner wisdom of our soul and not to others' random opinions. Death can be as individual as life.

24 June: 'I am Brave. There is Nothing to Fear'

Morgan starts to make his way towards the hall. His front legs give in. I immediately help him up. His front legs give in again. I sense a feeling of panic coming from him, as if he's trying to get away from something. He has fallen on his side and his panic is rising. I intuitively know he needs to be outside. I scoop him up and squeeze through the one open door to place him on the first bit of grass. He is immediately peaceful. I sit down with him and he starts to drift into a deep sleep. We stay like that for 30 minutes. I talk silently in my mind to him, telling him it's OK for him to ascend and that he doesn't need to stay here for anyone. I also tell him that I know I'll be OK when he's gone. I truly feel this now. Months earlier, even last year, it felt as though I would never reach this point, but I am so grateful I have, because with this knowing comes a wonderful sense of peace. Maybe it will only be temporary, but for now it was very comforting.

I tell Morgan I want him to choose what is best for him and what he needs.

Keeping his eyes closed, he tells me, 'I am brave. There is nothing to fear.'

'Are you going now?' I ask him, with wet cheeks.

'Not now. Recharging.'

This is all I need to know. I relax with him while he sleeps, just enjoying the moment – such an exquisite moment. He snoozes in the sunshine and Texas snoozes in his long-grass den behind us. We are all content.

26 June: Contemplating Life

The first day of a heatwave and the temperature is about 30 degrees. Morgan wants to spend time alone. I feel animals often want to review their life and before they transition they can often be observed in deep thought or a trance-like state, as though they are elsewhere at that moment. It seems to me that Morgan is also contemplating his life and thinking about his future.

27 June: Disagreeing over Quality of Life and Timing of Death

Yet again Jo and I have been at loggerheads about Morgan's quality of life and the timing of his death. She feels we should have got a vet to put him to sleep two weeks ago. She struggles to get past the external, outward appearance. I wish she'd trust me when I say Morgan tells me he doesn't want to go yet.

The Beginning of July

Jo and I have just found common ground. She is spending longer at home and realizes that on the rollercoaster of good and bad days Morgan is a dog keen to live – and eat chicken – for as long as he can. She's also starting to receive communication from him and when we ask him a question about his care she'll receive the same answer as me.

My gentle friend is clear he wants to hang on to life. He values life. He desires it. He told me late one night after I'd carried him upstairs and put him into his bed, 'Better to have some life than none at all.'

Mid-July: No More Medicine

Morgan wants us to stop giving him homoeopathic medicine. He wants it all to stop. No more invention. No more acupuncture. No more external support. I am aware that animals ask for medical and healing intervention to cease when they are close to transitioning. I feel he has started separating from his body and is beginning to let go. There are moments when he doesn't feel present and I'm aware he's spending time out of his body as pure energy.

22 July: Freedom

I have a workshop to teach in Snowdonia, but I don't want to leave home. I want to stay with Morgan because I feel there is not much time left. Jo reassures me he will still be here when I get back. I know this in my heart, but I have a deeper feeling that when I get back he will be ready to go. One part of me feels this trip to Wales is dreadful timing and the other surrenders and has faith in the universe guiding events for a reason.

On the way to Snowdonia I am curious to know *why now?* I get out my pack of Steven Farmer's Power Animal divination cards. There are 44 in the pack, but I feel drawn to one in particular. When I turn it over I read 'Freedom' and it has the image of a white horse. I immediately think of Morgan's freedom – freedom from his body to continue his soul's journey. My Welsh venue is called 'White Horses'. Rather than random chaos, it feels as though everything is as it's meant to be.

The next part of the book focuses on knowing when it's time. In the first chapter, Benson, a fell pony, answers his guardian's question: 'Did I choose the right time for him to leave us?'

Part III
WHEN IT'S TIME

'To every thing there is a season, and a time to every purpose under the heaven: a time to be born and a time to die.'
ECCLESIASTES 3:1

Chapter 9
'My Ears Don't Hurt' Benson

∽◦〜

*'She's in grief. It is deep. Natural. You can be there
for each other, share your grief. In silence. No words
needed – just a sharing of emotion. That is what love is.'*
BENSON

Benson, mostly known as Benny, was bought from a family in Cheshire. He came into Caroline's life with the plan that he'd live with her sister's family once they'd relocated to the countryside. Even though as a black Fell pony he was just 13.2 hands high, over the following 17 years he was to become the biggest influence on Caroline's life.

Caroline had attended a couple of my 'Introduction to Animal Communication' workshops but requested a communication with Benson because she felt her emotions were preventing her from connecting with him since he had passed over.

There is no shame in asking another person to communicate with your animal. Sometimes the issue is so important or the velocity of emotion so strong that a neutral unconnected experienced animal communicator is exactly what you need.

When I looked at Benson's picture I discovered kind deep brown eyes, a cheeky mischievous mouth and bedraggled hair sweeping down a smoky-black face. Grey flecks ran through his charcoal coat. When I connected with him I found him to be sweet, sensitive and thoughtful. I could also feel he was very deep-hearted: he just wanted to be loved and to give love.

Benny gave me a feeling of bliss as he pictured Caroline grooming him. He gave the impression he loved to have his hair brushed over his forehead, because at the same time Caroline would whisper sweet words of affection to him. I could sense he was her shoulder to lean on. He was a very kind pony and he could be fun too. He showed me that he loved to make mad dashes with his companion horse, Heather, who was grey coloured. He especially enjoyed going out hacking with Caroline. He told me he used to be with a child and they had entered gymkhanas. Proudly, he showed me his winning rosettes and a video-clip of himself going very fast. I could sense he loved speed and found it exciting. He then pictured a blue rug and a black saddle and Caroline holding his head and kissing his face.

Caroline confirmed that Benny had been ridden by a 13-year-old and had won many rosettes at gymkhana competitions. He did love to go fast and enjoyed hacks with her. Heather was indeed a grey horse and Benson's rug had been blue and his saddle black. Everything else made sense too.

We arranged a telephone appointment and Caroline began with the most important question of all: 'Did I choose the right time for him to leave us?'

'You know in your heart of hearts – yes,' Benny replied softly.

'Would he have wanted to carry on until September or October? I had already agreed with the vet that he wasn't up to another winter living out, even with his thick rugs, and he would have hated to be stabled.'

Many guardians ask me a similarly worded question. 'Could they have gone on longer?' 'Did I end their life too soon?'

'It wasn't to be,' Benny answered simply, in an accepting way.

Caroline's other concern was Heather, who wasn't her horse, but Benny and Heather had spent every minute of every day together for six years.

'She understands what has happened,' Caroline explained, 'because we let her be there when Benny died, but now she has shut down in grief and cut herself off from everything and everyone around her.'

Benny advised, 'Just let her be free. Let her work it out. She's in grief. It is deep. Natural. You can be there for each other. Share your grief. In silence. No words needed – just a sharing of emotion. This is what love is.'

'Does he have any messages for me about my life path?' Caroline said.

Benny immediately responded, 'Purple. I want you to develop your psychic abilities more. To study. To practise. To practise mediumship.'

'He wants to be in contact with you,' I explained, 'because he believes you need him and he loves you. He says you lack confidence. He wants you to make a real effort to do this for him. Dedicate the next three months to connecting with your "purple" chakra. Then he will talk with you and all will be well again. He doesn't want you to feel disconnected.'

After the communication Caroline wrote to explain how her bond with Benson had developed:

'I was quite nervous the first time I rode him out down the country lanes. I had been used to highly strung horses and it took me weeks to relax and trust Benny. That first time out, a car came whizzing round a blind bend and did an emergency stop in front of us to avoid ploughing into a tractor coming in the other direction. The tractor was pulling a wagon loaded high with bales of hay, two of which fell off the top as it braked, one in front of Benny.

My old Arab horse would have disappeared into the next field with me on top in fright, but Benny stood stock still for a moment, looked down at the bale of hay and then proceeded to tuck in quite calmly. If there was one thing that Benny loved, it was his stomach.

I used to go to the local shops with him, tying him up outside the newsagent's quite happily. He used to mug the toddlers coming out of the shop for their chocolate bars and ice-lollies. I remember once finding him blissfully chewing a lollipop, the stick just poking out of his mouth, his eyes closed in ecstasy. I looked down at the young child standing by him and said: "Did you give my pony your lolly?"

"No," said the child solemnly. "Pony took lolly!"

I bought the child another one and Benny looked so pleased that I hadn't the heart to tell him off.

He had favourite stopping points where he knew he'd get offered a biscuit, a mint or a carrot by the house owners. Especially if he did his "Please feed me, I'm starving" trick, which involved raising his hoof, waggling it in the air and nodding his head in circles at the same time.

We would often stop off at my house on the way back from a ride and I would take him to my back garden and tie him up by the kitchen door to share tea and toast with me. One day I came downstairs to find that he had untied himself and was happily standing in the kitchen raiding the bread bin. It was a long and narrow kitchen and impossible to turn him round, so I had to lead him through the dining room and round the dining table to finally exit through the kitchen door. He didn't bat an eyelid. I could tell he just thought it was great fun.

*He was so much more than a pony to me – he was
a much-loved soul mate and friend. I rarely rode in
winter, so he used to get turned out instead, but come the
spring I could get straight back on him and there was
never a problem.'*

In early 2003 everything changed. Caroline developed a frozen
shoulder, which started from a simple bicep tendon injury.
Unable to drive and care for Benny, she asked a friend to look
after him. Without checking with Caroline first, the friend's sister
allowed her children to put Benny into weekly school lessons.
At this time nobody knew Benny's real age and believed he was
much younger than his true years. The lessons were too difficult
and caused problems with his back and hindquarters.

In late 2004 and throughout 2005, Caroline experienced
many bereavements: her younger sister and gran passed over
within days of each other, her much-loved cat died suddenly
and her partner's father died on the day of her sister's memorial
service. Finally, Caroline's partner lost his job, then his driving
licence, shortly after he left her, and she was unable to cope with
either his grief or her own. At this point a second frozen shoulder
started and was painful and debilitating. The slightest knock
or touch would have Caroline doubled up on the floor in pain.
Everything became too much and she had a breakdown: unable
to face the world, she rarely left her bed for a month.

'I needed Benny very much at this time,' she said, 'but, as
people do when full of grief, I cut myself off from everything and
everyone, including him.'

Then all of a sudden her friend said she couldn't look after
Benny any more. Caroline felt she was in no fit state to find a
place for him, so, despite feeling that it was the wrong thing
to do, she agreed he could go out on loan to her friend's sister
in Macclesfield.

For a while Caroline sank even further into depression, but then synchronicity struck when she bumped into her old friend Anne, who was searching for a companion for her horse, Heather.

'This encounter filled me with some hope and began to lift me out of my black mood. A month later I went up to Macclesfield with a trailer to bring Benny back down to live with Heather. He almost dragged me up the trailer ramp, he was so desperate to come home.

Heather was always very fussy about her companions, but she and Benny took to each other the moment we let him into her field.'

Now seeing Benny daily, Caroline realized something wasn't right. He was clearly uncomfortable, but she couldn't put her finger on it. Then on the kind of damp February day that is unforgiving to arthritic conditions, they went down a bridle-path slope and Benny bucked. He would never have bucked in the past.

This was the incident that led Caroline to discover Reiki healing and then animal communication through the late Julie Dicker, who informed her that Benny was much older than she'd been told – in fact he was 29 years old. She also explained the physical concerns that had caused him to buck.

'Julie's reading was my first taste of in-depth animal communication and it amazed me. I had spent my life tuning in to animals but I hadn't realized the depths of communication that were truly possible... I followed Julie's advice and Benny appeared much happier.'

Researching Benny's background, Caroline discovered he was indeed in his twenty-ninth year. She repeatedly apologized to him for putting him through so much, until he himself complained, 'Stop apologizing. Enough. Stop beating yourself up.'

Caroline retired Benny because of his health problems and he and Heather enjoyed a seven-acre field all to themselves, including a large shelter, automatic water trough and grass aplenty. They loved it and were never out of each other's sight.

Meantime, Caroline explored animal communication further and attended workshops: 'During this time I gave Benny healing and he encouraged me on my animal communication path.'

He also offered valuable emotional support:

'My dad died in the winter of 2010 after five years of mental and physical decline with Alzheimer's. Benny supported me through it; I would cry into his mane. I would sob in frustration about things that were happening in my life and how difficult it was looking after elderly parents. He was my rock: he gave me kisses; he wrapped his neck around my body in a hug; he told me what I should do, how to look at the situation differently and how to accept what was going on. He gave me the strength to help my mum with her grief and also deal with my own. He taught me how important it was to be in the present, not wrapped up in the past or worried about the future. He told me how to give help to others without giving too much of myself. He gave me the physical energy to keep going. Mostly he communicated in feelings and pictures, but sometimes I heard words. Sometimes he would nip my knee if he thought I was getting too introverted and caught up in a situation. It was his way of saying "Enough now!"'

Benny was going downhill physically, however.

'Benny began to tell me he couldn't be here forever and his time was coming. One day Anne told me Heather had communicated to her, "Benny will die in this field." I could

*see Heather growing sadder in spirit – she knew her
beloved friend was reaching the end of his time.'*

Winter 2011 was coming to an end and Caroline realized she
couldn't put Benny through another cold winter. On good days
he was his usual cheeky self, but on bad days he was grumpy and
very quiet.

'Once I asked him where it hurt.

*"Well, my ears don't hurt," he stoically replied, now 36
years old.*

*It was beneath his pride to give in, but I felt he was now
just here for me. He felt he couldn't depart because I needed
him so much.*

*After my dad passed, I developed my link to spirit and
heard him quite clearly. In the summer of 2012, Dad said to
me, "You've got to let him go."*

*I went away on a two-week holiday to Kefalonia and
wasn't worried because Benny seemed his normal self.
When I returned, I went down to the field to discover he
could hardly walk. Anne was about to call the vet. She
told me he'd declined very fast over the past 24 hours.
His back legs were now completely rigid and stiff and he
was crossing them over with every step. This had never
happened before, not even during his worst arthritis
attacks. When I was away he had no longer needed to hold
himself together and was letting go.*

*The vet came a couple of hours later and suggested Benny
was reaching the end of the line. But I still couldn't face
it. I wasn't ready. I felt Heather wasn't ready. It was all
happening so fast. To see if Benny could pull through, the
vet and I agreed to give him large doses of bute for seven*

days. I was willing him on with all my heart, but by the
following Monday he still couldn't cope, even with the high
dosage. It had become obvious that he wasn't going to pull
through this time.'

Looking into his eyes, Caroline said, 'Benny, my darling, please
don't hold on for me any longer if it's too much for you. I don't
want you to suffer more pain for me. Please tell me honestly – do
you want to go to spirit?'

Benny answered simply, 'Yes.'

'I asked the vet to come and he said he'd be over in a couple
of hours and would also arrange for the crematorium
truck. Anne and I spent those two hours with Benny, giving
healing and love. We took last photos and we tried to tell
Heather what was happening.

Normally when the vet arrived Benny would lead him on a
merry dance because vets were his least favourite humans,
but for the first time in his life he stood completely still and
allowed the vet to inject a sedative. I led him to the open
grass of his field for the last time and said my goodbyes
with tears rolling down my face.

Although it was mid-July, the weather was very damp
and cold, with that drizzly rain where you get wet through
without really noticing. When the vet gave the final
injection Benny dropped like a lead weight through water.
I kneeled on the grass beside him, held his head, stroked his
face and told him, "I love you. I miss you. Please find a way
to come back to me in a new body one day if you can. Be at
peace now. Run free again in spirit."

Gradually his heart slowed, then stopped, and I witnessed
a dance of light particles rising out of his body. His spirit
was leaving and Benny was at peace at last.'

Heather was in the field when Benny transitioned and was completely distraught. She nuzzled Benny's body and began frantically prancing round him, snorting, half rearing, running off and coming back again time after time. The vet gave her a sedative.

'We wanted to leave Heather with Benny's body for a couple of hours, but the crematorium truck arrived promptly. Within 15 minutes Benny's body was leaving the field. It was too soon for Heather, but we felt we had no choice and had to allow Benny's body to be taken.

When the crematorium truck had departed, Heather continued to be very worked up, prancing and snorting. A friend suggested she bring over one of her quiet horses from the farm opposite to keep her company, but Heather was completely devastated and lashed out at the horse over the dividing fence.'

The next day Anne moved Heather to her home to help her through her grief. Nevertheless, Heather was inconsolable – she paced her field in a teardrop shape for weeks and her depression and sadness were palpable.

'I used to stand crying into her neck. Together we grieved for the little black pony we had lost.

For a while I was still numb with pain... My grief was so deep, so dark and so black, I just couldn't make contact with Benny myself. I had completely shut down but I desperately wanted to hear from him. I needed to know if it had been the right time.'

This was the point when Caroline asked me to communicate with Benny.

Finally we arrived at her last question: 'Will he return to me in the future somehow?'

Benny answered with soothing grace and reassurance, 'In spirit form I will be by your side always. But my lifetime with you is complete and it was perfect. Anything more would be greedy on both our parts. Trust in my love for you... Reassure Heather I am still here – alive – in spirit form. Find a dog or cat to love, as I have loved you.'

Later Caroline reflected:

The communication helped me so much. Everything Pea said was highly accurate. The reality was I had been beating myself up, thinking that I had taken Benny's life from him too soon. Yet, as Pea suggested, I took a look at a photo of Benny on his last day and I knew then I had made the right decision. I could see it in his face. It was like a warm feeling coming over me – a "right" feeling. The weather had turned wet and cold and there were floods. Benny would have been miserable. It was absolutely right that I hadn't let him suffer any longer.

Although I was in tears after I came off the phone to Pea, they were tears of relief. I was reassured that Benny was still with me and all I had to do was let go of the blackness and he would be able to reach me again.

In the following days, as my grief softened to sadness, Benny started to connect and there was a moment when I could even feel his warm breath in my ear. Over in the field I stood under the tree by the hedge that he loved for itching satisfaction and I heard him say: "This is where I want my ashes scattered."'

A new companion was discovered for Heather. Anne came across a pony she called Bella, a brood mare who had been beaten, underfed, overworked and abandoned. She accepted her on loan and put her in the adjoining field. The two girls got on extremely well and Heather began to care for the broken mare, just as she was broken in her grief.

Having experienced so much loss herself, Caroline had one more insight to share:

> 'When we lose loved ones, be they human or animal, we have to remember that they did more than just die – they lived. So much better to remember how they lived and the happiness shared than to wallow in the dark grief and get stuck focusing on their passing.
>
> Benny continues to guide me. I remember Pea had said he could do more for me in spirit than in body and this is proving to be the case. I am nearly ready to return to work as a healer and animal communicator and it is thanks to Benny, both in his life and in spirit form, that I am able to do so.'

Though our beloved animals will always care for us and guide us, it isn't easy to let them go. In the next chapter I share the moment Morgan told me he was ready to go and the ways I honoured and celebrated his life before his transition. With the purpose of helping others facing their own grief, I also share the brave, and not so brave, ways in which I faced his death.

Chapter 10
Morgan: Letting Go

❧

I knew before I went to Wales that once I got back Morgan would start letting go. How did I know? It was just a gut feeling. A knowing. We hadn't communicated it this time. We didn't need to.

On the first two train journeys back to London I sobbed quietly as I looked out of the window, vaguely registering countryside and houses. I was listening to music and aware of random lyrics about letting go. I knew straightaway these would be the tracks I played for Morgan as he let go and ascended. The third and last part of the train journey I tried to read a book as distraction, but there were those words time and again – 'letting go'.

I walked through the door of my home about 9 p.m., after a five-and-a-half-hour journey, feeling emotionally drained. Morgan had struggled to his feet and found the strength to walk into the hall, where he stood waiting for me, leaning against the wall for balance. I walked towards him, registering how frail he had become.

'I am ready now,' he said.

It was clear. I heard the words inside my head in my own inner voice, but the tone was his, the character behind the words was his. Morgan had told me what I'd been anticipating for the past six months.

Silent, I kneeled down, gently took him into my arms and held him close to my chest.

OK, I said silently in my mind. Knowing he'd made his decision.

He had asked and I would honour his wish. I had been honouring his wishes against the views of some friends and even my own partner at times, and I wouldn't falter now.

25 July 2011: Gratitude

This morning Morgan lies on the duvet in the living room and I hand feed him some white fish. He takes it, but with a hint of desperation, the whites of his eyes bulging. After setting up some bedding on the sofa, I lift him up to lie with me, his head alongside my leg. With my hand resting gently on the softness of his head, I thank him for being in my life.

He closes his eyes and relaxes into a very peaceful sleep, breathing softly beneath my hand, his chest very gently rising and falling and his beautiful dark brown eyelashes closed shut.

I feel unable to speak to the vet to arrange an appointment, but Jo offers to make the call.

Later in the afternoon I pull out the essential oil candles I purchased in Glastonbury especially for this time: the black one for protection, the white one for peace and the green one for love. I thank Morgan for everything he has shared with me and remind myself why he has been so significant in my life:

I am grateful for Morgan's presence in my life because:

He is so gentle.
He is very patient.
He has loved me unconditionally.

He has caused me to change my life.

He has caused me to look at myself.

He has caused me to look at my beliefs.

He has helped me to become a better person.

He has given me the strength to help many animals.

He has given me the strength to help many guardians.

He has given me the strength to share my knowledge and love of animals with others so that they can go on to improve the lives of the animals they love.

He has reminded me of the importance of happiness.

He has helped me reconnect with nature.

He has introduced me to people I would not have chosen to meet.

He has shown me pure love beaming from his deep soulful eyes.

Jo has an overnight work trip, so this is my last night with Morgan when it's just the two of us.

26 July

Today is our last day. I am sitting typing my feelings and the unfolding of Morgan's story as he has instructed, while he is lying in his bed across the room snoozing quietly.

Tomorrow the vet will come and help release him from his body.

As I write that line he struggles to his feet and comes over to me. I can feel he wants to be held, so, covering his weeping wart in a towel, I pick him up and put him on my lap. We stay like this for 90 minutes. He relaxes and goes to sleep. I softly stroke the thin white hair across his rib-prominent chest. I stroke all four legs and hold his paws. I am savouring the moment. In his younger, more vibrant years he would never have tolerated this level of contact. I stroke his ears. Admire his black button nose. And I listen to his breathing, feel his heart beat under my hand

and think about letting him go. Tomorrow he will no longer be in his physical body and what will be left behind will be purely his shell – discarded like a cocoon when a butterfly has flown free.

The phone rings and breaks our bliss. It's Jo, asking me to pick her up from the train station. She's returning from the press night of her show and I've asked her to pick up some flowers.

Morgan is now asleep, leaning his body against my leg. It feels peaceful and I feel so connected with him that I don't want to move. Jo amiably agrees to get the bus some of the way and I agree to pick her up closer to home.

I have become so used to Morgan having an awareness of external events that I'm not in the least surprised when he asks to get down a few moments after Jo requests collection. Settling him on his duvet bed on the floor, I close the door to prevent him struggling up the step to the kitchen, grab the keys and lock the door.

He is still cosy and asleep when we return less than five minutes later. Jo has bought up the flower shop and has her arms laden.

2:56 p.m.: Countdown

The clock counts down. The time is approaching when Morgan will be given the drug that will stop his heart and end his dear life. My hero, my mentor, my best friend. The agony feels so intense, I feel myself breaking into bits, flying in every direction. I feel lost.

Jo arranges three large vases of flowers. There are sunflowers, daisies, tall pure-white blossoms and many flowers in lilac, purple and indigo. She has gone all out, no expense spared.

I place two vases in the fireplace on either side of the candles then gather all the rose quartz crystal in the house and scatter the pink tumble stones around the candles.

'I like it,' Morgan tells me from where he rests on his bed.

I want to make it perfect for him, a peaceful shrine. On the mantelpiece I place four gold-painted china letters that spell LOVE, more candles, a soft toy dog in Union Jack material which I bought months before when we were on 'Morgan's last holiday' down in Kent, a gold pot beautifully decorated with birds and flowers, and his photo, the one where he is beaming the biggest smile, his eyes sparkling with happiness. His true essence shines out from the picture frame. I wonder if I have done enough to make it right for him.

'I like it,' he tells me again. His communication is short but clear.

I play relaxing music to help us all stay calm, different CDs by Bliss. The lyrics fill my eyes with tears of both sorrow and joy.

My desire is to keep everything relaxed so that Morgan can enjoy his final day incarnate on Earth. I try and focus on the relief he will feel when he lets go of his body and remind myself it is his decision and his timing.

Lucinda Drayton's beautiful tones sing out again: 'Got to keep the faith, keep your faith in love.'

I spend a moment letting my Facebook friends know that Morgan will be transitioning. Many have been asking after him and know I have been a devoted carer over the past few months. People like to help, as that is human nature, so I offer a suggestion which I know will fit well with Morgan's own wishes: 'I invite you to light a candle for Morgan and send loving rose-coloured light. This light will carry the vibration of the heart chakra and support his transition.'

27 July: Transition Day

I am up with Morgan a few times in the night. At 4 a.m. he wants to go downstairs. I put on my robe, gather him into my arms and carry him down. There's a sense of urgency from him and before we reach the last step he can no longer control his bladder. I hold him tightly and whisper, 'It's OK.'

In the kitchen he's not interested in eating very much. He's tired. He knows what day it is. I try hand feeding him chicken. He accepts, but has no desire to eat directly from his bowl.

Afterwards I place a duvet on the sofa and lift him on. He immediately relaxes, lying on his right side, his head closest to me. I stroke him gently and he drifts off to sleep. Every now and again he wakes and I reassure him I'm with him and he's OK. We stay like this for hours. Time ticks on from 4 a.m. to 5 a.m., then from 6 a.m. to 7 a.m. I see the clock counting down and it feels surreal, as if I'm observing it but not really taking part.

I have the desire to write Morgan a letter explaining how incredibly special he is and why I feel so grateful that he is in my life. I want to put my feelings onto paper. Resting my left hand on his shoulder, I write them all down. My heart goes into every word. Occasionally I pause to think and feel before resuming. I want to give this to Morgan as an expression of my love.

Jo wakes up and comes to join us.

'I'm writing a letter to Morgan to let him know everything he means to me. Maybe you'd like to do this too?'

She agrees, and while I am showering she sits with Morgan and composes her own words in a card. I notice there is a Chinese symbol on the front and under it one word: 'Tranquillity'.

We take it in turns to sit with Morgan on the sofa and to make cups of tea. We oven-cook some more chicken and the smell wafts into the room. Morgan decides he wants to get down from the sofa and after a comfort visit to the garden manages to walk, completely unaided, through the living room into the hall, receives a bit of a hand up the step and then continues unaided into the kitchen, where he stands still.

'Chicken,' I feel him request.

Jo cuts it up while I steady him. She starts to hand feed it to him and he takes it with great enthusiasm. But then he takes us both unawares by walking over to his empty food bowl.

'He wants it in his bowl!' I say, surprised.

We oblige and he amazes us further by standing all by himself and eating every last piece. We both know this isn't a gesture of wanting to continue, this is a last-ditch effort to eat as much of his favourite food as he can, with as much dignity as possible, before he says goodbye.

It's now 10:30 a.m. Even though we've been up since 4 a.m., the time has flown past. It's time for Jo to head over to the veterinary surgery to bring the team back to our home. The vet doesn't have a car, so this is the one condition of the home visit.

Morgan wanted a home visit and so did we. He was always anxious at the vet's. We also preferred his last moments to be somewhere he felt comfortable, especially as we had the gift of time to make the arrangements.

Jo and Morgan have a moment together then she picks up the car keys and leaves. I lie on the floor opposite him in front of our very large mantelpiece set up like an altar with the candles, incense and flowers. Looking into his eyes and holding his left paw in my hand, I feel tears streaming gently across my face and into my hair.

'I love you. I love you. I love you,' I repeat like a mantra. 'You are a great dog.'

I explain what is going to happen and that all he has to do is let go. We lie like this for a few minutes then I start to feel panicky. What if it goes wrong? What if he feels pain? I am suddenly fearful and reach out for guidance from my pack of Doreen Virtue's Archangel Michael cards. I spread the deck out picture face down and out of a pack of 44 I discover I've chosen 'God is in Charge'. The saying that goes with the card is a prayer and I read it then say it out loud:

'Dear God, please help me let go of this situation, giving it in faith and trust to your Divine wisdom and infinite love in order to resolve and heal everything and everyone involved.'

I feel an immediate sense of peace descend and wonder how I could ever have doubted that Morgan would be in safe hands.

I lie back down with him, calm again. I hold his paw, look into his eyes and repeat my words of love and gratitude.

He makes a move to get up and I help him until he is balanced on his feet. I gently support him as he goes towards the back door and out into the garden. Looking back, I can see he was aware Jo was returning with the vet and nurse.

The weather is beautiful – bright and sunny with a pale blue sky and cool air. Morgan turns right out of the door to take a long drink from his stainless-steel water bowl, makes his way onto the lawn, wobbling up the right side beside the railway sleepers, and empties his bladder at the top. He then loops around to the left and starts to wobble his way back down the lawn towards the middle of the garden. I realize he wants to transition here, so I take his pale blue fleece off the clothes line and spread it out on the lawn. Morgan topples towards it and sits there, then lies down. I feel he has decided – this is where he wants to be: on the earth, under the sky, surrounded by trees and plants. Sitting beside him, I take his paw in my hand and stroke the top of his head, knowing he will never stand again.

Over and over again I tell him how special he is. 'I love you. I love you.'

At some point the doorbell rings.

I kiss him and say, 'OK, my darling, they're here. They're going to help you transition.'

It had always been our wish that he would die peacefully in his sleep. Isn't it everyone's wish? But Morgan was too frail, too worn out. He'd tried. He'd tried on Monday and I'd called in Light from above and visualized him leaving his body and ascending, but it wasn't to be. Just before he'd gone out into the garden, when I was lying on the floor holding his paw and waiting for Jo to bring the vet, I felt he'd tried to ascend for a second time. He'd closed his eyes and tried to drift by himself. Jo had even thought she might arrive with the vet to be told his services were no longer needed.

I remember the walk to the door to let them in. Jo had deliberately not taken a key so I'd have notice of their arrival. As I walked towards them, time seemed to slow down. I remember understanding that when I opened that door it wouldn't be long before Morgan was no longer physically with me. I had to force myself to put one foot in front of the other.

Opening the door, I could only muster 'Hello' before I turned and walked back to Morgan. I hadn't wanted to leave him even for a second, but he was exactly where I'd left him. Even when the vet and nurse joined us, he didn't move. He didn't lift his head. He barely moved his eyes. He was just waiting, perfectly still and knowing.

I checked the procedure with the vet who, to our great disappointment, wasn't Morgan's usual vet but a locum, because Morgan's vet had broken for his summer holiday just days before. I hadn't wanted the locum – someone I didn't know and who didn't know Morgan. I'd even picked up the cards for guidance on this, but before I'd even spread the deck out I was stopped by Morgan's reassurance: 'The locum will be fine.' If he felt OK about it then I would too. We have to accept we can't always control everything, even with the best will in the world.

The locum very briefly explained what he was going to do, I questioned him on it and then he gave me more details. He wanted to get straight to it, but that felt wrong to me – disrespectful.

'Morgan is telepathic. Can you explain to him everything you're going to do?'

'Telepathy is thoughts, isn't it?' he replied.

'Yes, that's right, but if you can still say the words out loud then there'll be pictures behind your thoughts and he'll understand what you're going to do,' I said to him, thinking *Please don't question me on this.* I didn't know this man, but I wanted to be sure that he saw Morgan as a sentient being and gave him due respect rather than seeing this as just a job where he was indiscriminately 'putting someone's pet down'. If it had been Morgan's regular vet I wouldn't have needed to say anything because he understood and knew about animal communication.

The locum shaved a few inches of hair off Morgan's left front leg then prepared the needle. It was filled with a vivid blue liquid and measured according to Morgan's weight. Jo stroked his neck while I looked into his eyes and stroked his side. The locum explained what he was going to do and then inserted the needle into Morgan's vein and slowly pushed the liquid in. Within a second Morgan stretched his head back and the needle jerked and fell out and in that moment I knew – he had gone.

The vet seemed surprised, as he'd pushed in less than half of what he felt was needed. But I put my hand on Morgan's heart and for the first time I didn't feel a thing.

'He's gone,' I whispered, barely able to speak.

The locum got his stethoscope out and listened. After a short moment he confirmed that Morgan was no longer with us and reiterated he was amazed how little of the drug had been needed.

It was no surprise to Jo and me. Morgan had only needed a slight helping hand. His energy was flat. He was worn out. He'd decided to let go and, more importantly, he'd said he was ready. It was his wish, his divine timing. We weren't expecting him to fight the additional help. We only wished for his transition to be gentle.

So many different sources were supporting him. Some of his human friends and our students and clients had lit candles and sent healing love, and some animal friends in the place we call heaven, including his previous guardians, who were in spirit, did whatever they do to help a soul transition.

Morgan had gone home. He was flying free now, flying home.

His eyes were open but he wasn't behind them. They were vacant. He was very, very still. It was about a minute later that I remembered to ask the time.

'It's 11:12,' the vet said.

So it had been 11:11 a.m. when Morgan had ascended. I'd wondered whether he would go then. I hadn't got a watch on, but I wasn't surprised that the timing would work out for Morgan to ascend at 11 minutes past 11 in the year 2011. He had transitioned on a Balsamic Moon day, which represents endings, particularly relationship endings.

We exchanged pleasantries with the vet and nurse. Neither Jo nor I remember what they said to us. Jo drove them back to the surgery. I wouldn't have had the strength. I don't know how she did it.

I stayed with Morgan. I put my arms around his body and very quietly sobbed into his hair. I stroked his head and kissed him time and again. My beautiful boy had gone. I looked into his eyes but he wasn't there. It was just his shell. I missed his presence immediately. My heart broke, shattering into thousands of pieces, scattering in the wind.

It was silent. Peaceful. I didn't hear my neighbours, I didn't hear any traffic, I didn't hear the birds. I engaged with the silence. It was like hearing stillness, if that is possible. It was just Morgan and me. Together, out on the grass, in the soft sunshine. It was as if time had stopped.

Part IV
GRIEVING IN PROGRESS

*'I realize there's something incredibly
honest about trees in winter, how
they're experts at letting things go.'*
JEFFREY McDANIEL

Chapter 11
Morgan: The First Time

The first time I wake up late: 8:15 a.m.

The first time I look down to where Morgan would be in his bed, barely inches away from me. Empty. No bed. No Morgan.

The first time I walk downstairs in the morning not carrying Morgan in my arms, trying to get him to the back garden before nature calls.

The first time I'm not holding him steady while he eats.

The first time I'm not helping him walk, supporting him as he wobbles, or carrying him back to the living room to place him gently on his bed.

The first time I'm sitting on the sofa without him lying on the half-folded duvet on the floor.

The first time I'm sitting here and his bed is not where it should be.

I hate this feeling. I hate this empty space. I miss him so much. I miss his eyes and soft face. I miss his beautiful presence in my home. He has changed my life in so many ways.

Caring for him virtually every day for the past six months has opened my heart wider than I ever thought possible. We were so close, so in tune. My heart was bursting with unconditional and all-encompassing love for him. As he grew weaker, my love intensified. I knew I would do anything for him.

Sitting here without him now is the worst feeling. The biggest and most loving influence in my life has died.

I feel numb.

I pick up his photo and burst into tears.

'Write it all out,' I hear him tell me.

But now I don't know if I am just making it up. Is it just my mind wanting to hear this or is it really Morgan telling me what to do? Without Morgan's physical presence, doubt has crept in.

Silence.

8:44 a.m. We would have been up together, just the two of us, for about five hours now. So much time spent together. Now nothing. I want to lift him onto the sofa next to me.

Jo and I grieve in a different way. I am busy being; Jo is busy doing. She cleans. She pulls up the off-cuts of carpet. This is her way. She tells me she looks down to where Morgan's bed would have been and sees him lying in it peacefully with a smile on his face. She sees the positive rather than the pain. She experienced death when she was a child and her family taught her that it was a positive rather than a negative experience. She was told death wasn't the end and that 'loved ones look over you and will be with you all your life'. So her outlook on death has always been incredibly optimistic. I grew up with media and books informing me that death was a very traumatic thing and in a family where tears of grief were hidden.

Regrets start piling in on top of one another. I wish I had spent more time with Morgan. I wish I hadn't gone away to teach in Wales.

12:55 p.m. His bedding has been put in a pile. All the towels and covers have been washed. Most are dry; some are hanging on the line in the sunshine. It feels fast. Yet I've been expecting this moment for months.

Jo is the most grounded and practical person I know. She does not outwardly cry over things that matter and told me she wouldn't over Morgan. She still hasn't shed one tear; I have wept an ocean. Neither is wrong, neither is right. It's not that she doesn't feel or didn't adore Morgan. She's a true dog person and instigated Morgan coming into our lives. She just copes in another way.

My emotions flood out of me. I look at Morgan's photos and remember all the moments we shared. I think of him in my life and feel his absence. The house is empty without him. I need silence. No music. No TV. No noise. I am feeling completely overwhelmed.

8:30 p.m. Two remaining candles, love and peace, are burning brightly. Beside them is a tube in a sleeve of pretty bluebells within a forest of trees. In the tube are the ashes of Morgan's body. 'His skeletal remains,' the cremator has informed us. The rose quartz tumble stones now surround the tube and this peaceful scene brings me comfort. I replay yesterday over and over in my mind and recall the magical moments.

The loss of an animal is a very real and relevant cause for grief. I am sharing my day-to-day grieving process in the wake of Morgan's death to help you understand that you are not alone and there are others who share your depth of sadness.

Light Joining Light

Jo took about 15 minutes to drop the veterinary team off. Within that time some magical and unexpected things happened.

When I was alone with his body I asked Morgan, 'Where are you?'

I heard his voice come back to me, 'Still journeying.'

At least, I thought, *he is on his way.*

Before Jo had brought the vet to our home I'd said to Morgan, 'When you've gone, please give me a sign that you're OK. Let me know you're all right.'

I had presumed this would take a number of days – time for him to journey and then get used to his new existence without a body. However, before Jo returned, and without even asking for contact, I was shown an image in my mind's eye. I could see Morgan full of joy and barking – barking with happiness – and young again. I could see him vibrant and full of strength, no longer skin and bones and struggling to walk. Either side of him I could see lots of animals – too many to count. I had a feeling of him being flanked by two of my canine pals who were also in spirit. I wondered who all the other animals were and how Morgan could know so many.

I loved the image, but it took me by surprise. It was so quick. Many people say the soul takes hours to leave the body. Still, I knew Morgan had been ready and it had taken only the slightest injection for him to rocket out of his body and upwards to the light. His shift in energy had been very strong and intentional. So I wanted to believe in the picture, but I found it hard, not only because of the speed of its delivery but because right beside me was Morgan's body.

'Trust it,' I heard loud and clear from Morgan – a gentle instruction. It came from the air around me, not the body lying on the grass.

I want to trust it, I thought. *I really do, but what if I'm just making it up to give myself some comfort? How do I know it's real?*

'Trust it,' I heard Morgan tell me again.

'You couldn't trust it,' Jo pointed out to me later.

She was right. I needed confirmation that Morgan's soul had left before we took his body to the crematorium. So I used a technique I teach my students when they are learning how to move their consciousness inside an animal to sense what they are feeling. I moved my consciousness inside Morgan's head.

It's hard to put feelings in to words sometimes, but what I felt in the dead body of my best canine friend was *nothing*. Just *nothingness*. He wasn't there. To be sure, I moved down to his heart, which I found to be completely still, and then into his general chest area. Everything was still. His body was vacant. Empty. The spirit had literally departed and only the casing and mechanics were left.

I imagine some people will think this morbid or outlandish, but I needed to be sure Morgan's soul had left before we took his body to be cremated. I really needed this extra confirmation.

Then the next miracle happened. In my mind's eye I could see a black dog far off in the distance. There were no other details – I couldn't tell what breed or what sex, I just knew it was a black dog. I wondered whether this could be the dog Morgan had told me about before he transitioned. One day I had been thinking about Morgan's absence and I heard him tell me, 'We are sending someone to you.'

I had come to realize by then that Morgan did not work alone. He supported me and in turn was supported by a team of beings. Some I felt were animals and some either people or angelic-type beings. Now I knew they were sending someone to me.

Out on the lawn I put my arms around Morgan. I kiss his ruff and gently sob into his soft white hair. At some point during this he says, 'That's not me. I've gone.' Even straight after his own transition he is reassuring me.

Two hours pass very quickly. Jo and I spend it outside with Morgan's body, sometimes stroking him and talking about him, but mostly sitting in silence, swinging from feeling shocked and hollow to feeling peace in our hearts and glad that we have honoured Morgan's wishes.

Then we have to get ready to go to the crematorium. We decide to take Morgan in his soft oval bed. We line it with a cream blanket. Jo prepares some flowers to go with his body. I gather the letters we wrote thanking him for being in our lives, two pink roses and two rose quartz crystals. This is agony, but we are calm and united.

Jo picks up Morgan's body and his head flops down. I hold it and balance it in her arms and she carries Morgan out to the back of our car and places him gently in his bed. He is draped in his small red fleece with black and white paw prints. It covers his body but reveals his head and the ruff of his neck. He looks peaceful, as though he's simply asleep.

Over the course of the drive his facial expression changes. In the back garden he looked old, frail and no longer present. Now his whole presence has turned very soft, even cosy, and there is a large smile on his face. He looks as though he is having a wonderfully happy dream. The change is quite remarkable. The sight of his newly relaxed and cheerful expression in turn soothes our anxiety and we know, deep down, all is well.

We arrive at the crematorium 15 minutes early. The owner, Kevin, comes out to meet us. He tells us the Farewell Room isn't quite ready. We are in no rush. Morgan looks so content in his bed and we don't want to move him. We certainly don't want to take the next steps, although we know they are necessary.

When the Farewell Room becomes available, Jo lifts Morgan up from his bed and carries him inside. Kevin takes his bed and I bring our letters and the flowers and crystals. Morgan is still smiling.

As Kevin talks about the crematorium ethics and approach, Morgan lies in his bed on a table behind me and I stroke his paw and tell myself, This is not him, this is not him, he's gone, it's only his body.

I remain focused on the image of Morgan barking and surrounded by friends. I keep my heart tight shut. I go through the motions. I talk about the paperwork. What will be going with Morgan's body and what won't. We are taking his bed and bedding home to donate to the animal home that saved his life and allowed us to adopt him. I am keeping his collar, even though he hasn't worn it for some months. Going with him will be the flowers, the crystals and letters.

Kevin explains how it all works. We can choose the modern cremator or the old-fashioned one. We choose the old-fashioned one. He has already booked it out for us, so his instincts are in tune. We can attend Morgan and see his body put onto the steel tray then disappear inside the cremator kiln, or we can say goodbye to him in the Farewell Room and trust Kevin to take his body and treat him with respect. We choose this option. Neither of us wants the image of Morgan being lifted onto the cold tray or taken into the fire of the cremator. We want to remember him lying peacefully in his bed, snug and tucked up in his red fleece with that wonderful heartwarming smile on his face.

We are left alone to say our goodbyes. I say goodbye to Morgan, kiss him, tell him I love him and step back. Jo says her own goodbye and we leave the room. She has to visit the bathroom and leaves me waiting for her in the hall.

I am suddenly struck by the finality of this moment and slip back inside the room, where I kiss Morgan's head and soft brown left ear, grasping extra moments, feeling that I am being ripped apart. I have to force myself to leave, knowing I will never see or feel his beautiful, reassuring, happy, independent body ever again. This is the very final moment with Morgan as a physical being.

I go outside and wait for Jo in the car.

We have asked for an immediate return of Morgan's ashes. Kevin has said we can wait in Dignity's garden or go for a walk along a nearby canal. Close to the canal there is a pub where we can park up. Jo and I have discussed going for a long walk, but now we both want a drink and head to the pub instead.

It feels wrong being in a pub without Morgan. It's alien. A pub is a lonely place without a dog. Especially a dog who loves the crisps he'll get to share. I glance down and Morgan is no longer there waiting. He should be there. He loves pubs and always has. I'm sure before he came to us he lived with people who took him to the pub, as he's always been totally relaxed in them.

'I don't know how long I can live without a dog in my life,' I say to Jo.

She is taken by surprise. I've already explained that I want to spend the next year focusing on my workshops and teaching abroad, that we can both be freer without a dog for a while and that it will give us time to grieve and come to terms with our loss before welcoming a new, bright doggie being into our lives.

We sit outside with our drinks and the obligatory packet of crisps, but no Morgan. This feels awful. Dogs leave so many lasting memories in all the places we go.

All is Well

Back home I sit still. Remembering. I feel like a pendulum swinging between agony and peace. I feel deep grief that causes uncontrollable gut-wrenching cries of pain. I also know that all is well. Morgan needed to leave his body and the timing was perfect for him. We honoured his wish.

Chapter 12

Morgan: The Emotions
that Follow Loss

29 July 2011

_Can't eat. I felt numb on the ferry trip here to the Isle of Wight.
It felt as though it wasn't really happening and at some point I'd
wake up from this terrible nightmare and Morgan would be there
with smiling eyes and joy shining out from his body like golden
beams of light._

_Jo and I would bring Morgan on holiday here. We'd travel on a
ferry with a deck section for dogs and a doggie watering station
inside. Morgan was always a brilliant traveller, taking everything
in his stride. Life was one big adventure for him and he loved new
places and new smells._

_Off the ferry I meet two dogs: a Yorkshire terrier called Poppy
who makes a big fuss of me and is very happy, and a gentle collie
called Sky, who immediately feels my pain and licks my hands
over and over again as she looks, concerned, into my eyes._

I explain to her male guardians, 'I lost my dog two days ago.'

My words wobble before I manage to finish the sentence. I can see the men understand and are moved, but are struggling to find the right words in reply.

'He was 17 years old,' I tell them, knowing this will make it easier.

'That's a good age,' says the man closer to me.

I nod in agreement, as words are hard to say when you're trying to swallow tears. 'Have a good day,' is the most I can muster and I have to leave before the tears spring forth.

Only now do I see the significance of the dogs' names – Poppy being the flower of remembrance and Sky being where heaven resides. It feels like a sign.

I have retreated to Stewart's island home. Stewart is a Maine Coon cat who came to me via clients, Belinda and Laura. Over the years I helped him he brought me and his two female guardians closer together and had a profound effect on my life that continues to this day. He transitioned in 2009.

When we arrive at our friends' home we find a card waiting for us with an image on the front of a dog outline similar to Morgan. There are also some flowers and part of the bunch is a single rhododendron bloom. Jo bought exactly the same colour of rhododendron for Morgan. It is in a vase back home. This feels like another gentle confirmation that we're in the right place at the right time.

I note the colours of the bouquet are the higher chakra colours: indigo, violet and white. I wonder whether they were requested or if the florist put them together by coincidence. Again, this feels symbolic, because now Morgan is in a higher realm, living a higher-vibrational existence.

Someone e-mails me an image of a pink rose, the colour of the heart chakra and a symbol of love.

Online I read the Daily Good message: 'Turn your wounds into wisdom' – Oprah Winfrey.

So many things feel like messages or signs from Morgan, perfectly orchestrated.

30 July

Leaving our home and coming away to our friends' house has removed us from the intensity of emotions and memories at home. I walk past a life-like drawing of Stewart and hear 'He's OK, you know.' I recognize his voice and know he is referring to Morgan.

However, I still have no appetite. Eating, walking and talking are all too much. It is a struggle to do anything. I make myself go through the motions of normal life.

It's hard to grieve with your partner when you grieve in a different way. Jo wants to go out and do things. I want to sit and write about Morgan, reflect and contemplate. It helps me feel close to him.

She's left again to go to the shops. This time in a huff. She slammed the door on the way out, stating, 'I'm grieving too, you know!' She's really in a huff because she tried to buy me a present to cheer me up, but the credit card was rejected and we will be charged a fee – the act of kindness backfired.

Still, the slamming of the door feels like an assault. Everything feels overwhelming. I can hear a band drumming in the centre of Cowes, and although it is streets away, it is too loud. I need silence. I wonder how I can go on without Morgan. It feels too painful to stay here without him.

Later we go to the island's zoo so that I can visit Casper, the white lion, for guidance. We've met on previous visits to the island and I admire him greatly.

When I arrive at his enclosure he immediately beams white light into my heart from his third eye chakra.

'Be calm,' he instructs. 'We white lions will support you. You need a greater energetic support. Morgan did all he could.'

The underlying sense is Morgan did all he could within his means.

Casper's next message is: 'Love large'.

Then I feel him explain that a calm strong heart is a courageous heart.

His final message to me is: 'Find your lion-hearted courage.'

Raw, animalistic howls of grief again late this evening. Mine. It is hard to put what I feel into words; it's along the lines of having my solar plexus ripped out. It is the agonizing ripping ache of separation. It's physical and uncontrollable.

Now I will honour Morgan with the depth of my love and pain at our physical separation. I will have to find my lion-hearted courage tomorrow...

31 July

While I am lying outside in the sunshine, Morgan instructs me to write a book about animals going through the transition of death as a supportive guide for all animal lovers. He tells me the book is to include my personal journey with him and also true-life cases of my clients and their animals, based on animal communication and the animals' views of dying and death. I write the outline and chapter headings in about 30 minutes – all communicated by Morgan. It feels good.

When it comes time to leave the comfort of my friends' home, my emotions are triggered again. I gather up the photo of Morgan, the flowers and sympathy card. We have to go home now, but it's not home without him. It's empty and lifeless.

Yet I know I need to return for Texas. He needs his family too and not only has his environment changed now there are no bits of carpet and rug, but his canine companion and two human friends are missing too.

I have mixed emotions on the ferry back. I sit gazing out at the vastness of the sea and feel deep sadness at facing life without Morgan by my side, but I'm also looking forward to seeing Texas and gathering his furry ginger body up into my arms. I feel sure he'll be aware of our return and will be waiting for us.

As predicted, Texas runs up the centre of the road to our car the moment we park. It's great to see him. Understandably, he's out of sorts and takes a couple of hours to settle. We play with his mouse in the garden and feed him loads, and he helps make up a fresh bed through his normal trick of lying on it, like a resplendent lion king, while we're still trying to change the bottom sheet and duvet cover. For a moment, life feels normal, but then I glance to my side of the bed and there's empty space where Morgan's bed should be that echoes the emptiness in my heart.

1 August

Nothing feels right.

I light the white peace and green heart candles in the fireplace and a stick of incense. I feel numb again. The sun is shining brightly outside but not within me.

Jo has just walked in and commented, 'It feels so empty.'

Very. I can't believe I have to teach a course this Saturday. I don't know how I'm going to speak. Trust Morgan to transition just before the hottest day of the year and before my 'Empowering Animals' course for experienced students.

It's less than a week since Morgan ascended and I can still hardly eat. I can't talk to anyone. I don't want to do anything. Yet Jo continues with life. 'Because it's got to be done,' she tells me.

I don't want to be here.

2 August

I am very slowly beginning to accept what has happened, but there is a part of me that doesn't want to. I realize a part of me wants to stay in the agony of my loss because I don't want to accept that Morgan has gone. It's denial. I know it isn't healthy.

Life evolves – it changes and moves. Many animals have told me during communication that life is circular and this makes sense to me.

I begin to make sure the business that Morgan co-created continues to flow. Animal Thoughts is really his. I'm not sure many people would understand that. But part of my loss is that my business partner is no longer here with me. He was always helping me make decisions about which way to turn next.

At the moment he is having a rest. It sounds absurd writing it down, but RIP translates to 'He who rests in peace'. I've created a tribute page to Morgan on my website and when I find the words I'll add text there too. At the moment it's a picture of him sitting next to 'Special' graffiti and a picture of him in his favourite wood, chuffed to bits that he's found a discarded bone, which he's carrying around like a trophy, tail wagging joyfully from side to side.

Life continues and we go to the cinema to watch the final Harry Potter film. We chose not to go before so we could spend every last moment with Morgan, realizing his struggle was gaining momentum and his life force ebbing away. All through the film the theme is light versus dark. It reminds me of the Light that Morgan shines: always being positive and overcoming difficulties. The film ends and my automatic thought is We need to get back to Morgan.

As soon as I realize what I've thought, I start to sob. Between tears I struggle to tell Jo why I'm crying. She understands. Other people in the cinema probably think I'm crying because it's the end of the last Harry Potter film.

When I get home there is a message waiting:

'Dear Pea,

I was very moved by your message in the newsletter about dear Morgan. He was, is and will remain your best friend. That sounds a simple and understated way of describing such a special spirit who came into your life, but "friend" is a huge connection of love, which we are blessed with, and "best" friend therefore is the pinnacle of this love, which we share so rarely and with so very few.

My heart goes out to you at this moment because Morgan has a journey to travel of his own – as we shall all have to do when that time comes – however, when his journey is completed, you will find out that he is then able to be there with you at all times, wherever you go in this world. He has not gone; he will advise you with stronger and stronger messages and communications – I know that you do know this fact in your heart already, but it is still a painful time for you and all those who knew and loved Morgan as the spirit who walked this Earth.

Very soon you will start to see the little signs of his presence: he will make you laugh when you least expect it, he will give you the answer to something as you raise the question, he will run across your path when you are wondering which route to take.

All my love and thoughts to you and to Morgan, and thank you, Pea, for all the help and kindness that you show in communicating between the human spirit and the spirit of our beautiful animal friends across this strange, wonderful and sometimes difficult world. The only thing I can say is the best is yet to come for you and for Morgan – still with you, still communicating and now stronger than ever.

All my love,

Caroline x'

It was such a beautiful message, I was smiling when I replied:

'Thank you so much for taking the time to write this. I am so moved by it. Strangely, I went away at the weekend and ended up picking up a small wooden love heart with "best friend" written on it. I wasn't sure why, I was just drawn to it, but the thought of Morgan was there in my mind. I believe what you've written and Morgan has even made a little contact already, but the physical loss of him feels huge right now, as I was caring for him 24/7 for many months before he ascended.'

Caroline responded:

'Physical loss is huge. You are still caring for Morgan by wishing him a calm journey and giving him the gift of a warm, comfortable spot in your heart for his well-earned rest. I don't think it was strange you found the love heart from your "best friend" – he's telling you not to worry. He was here for a good long time and did everything asked of him. He may need a little peaceful nap right now, while still keeping you safe. He says, "Think of me as curled up asleep in my favourite spot. Go about your day with renewed energy and happiness. I will soon be awake, strong, refreshed and raring to go." What you can achieve together from then on will be absolutely amazing.'

3 August

One week to the day since Morgan ascended and 11:11 a.m. has come and gone unnoticed. I am on a train to Leeds to visit my adoptive mother, Mary. I am still struggling to be at home without Morgan. Jo is busy working on her designs for two shows and has no choice but to move forward. Yet she wants the TV on, I don't. She wants to play her music loud, I need complete silence.

A man in the seats next to me is on his mobile. He's been on it for over 20 minutes. Every cell in my body is screaming, 'Quiet!' I need silence. I foolishly think, Don't you know a very special dog has just died? I imagine this is how it feels for anyone who has just experienced a very significant loss. How can the rest of the world keep moving when my own world has fallen apart?

Grief comes out in different ways. Over the past two days I've had a 'dead' left arm – heavy, numb and aching. It feels as though something is trapped. I know it's my grief.

Mary understands how meaningful my relationship with Morgan was and how huge this loss is for me. This quiet understanding enables me to feel more able to laugh and smile today.

5 August

Thankfully the fog is lifting a little. Part of me welcomes the relief, yet part of me struggles to move forward because it feels like a betrayal of the significance of my loss. It's a funny thing, human nature.

I remind myself that one of Morgan's major roles in life was to be happy and he liked people around him to be happy too.

6 August

Arrived home from Leeds to more sympathy cards. These cards are a comfort, because people are acknowledging my grief. The first one has beautiful pink roses on the front and a comforting message inside. I also receive a real photo print of a yellow rose from neighbours who would regularly see me take Morgan into the woods for his morning walk. The pink and yellow roses feel like a sign that Morgan is still close and they warm my heart.

Signs are personal – you either feel a connection or you don't. When you do, the trick is believing it rather than questioning it all the time.

I have the workshop tomorrow. Attaching the course information to a group e-mail, I explain I will try not to let the students down.

Amanda sweetly replies:

'Dear Pea,

You could NEVER let us down. If you do not feel strong enough, you can take strength from us. We will be there to support you as you have supported us. Thinking of you,

Lots of love,

Amanda.'

7 August: 'Empowering Animals' Stage 1

Before I even step a foot through the church hall door, the thought strikes me: I wonder whether one of the students will bring me a rose as a sign from Morgan?

This London venue is where I'm to hold the first part of my 'Empowering Animals' animal communication course. I'm immediately struck by an empty feeling. Morgan's toenails aren't clattering across the wooden floor as he checks out every nook and cranny for tasty morsels. It's my first workshop without my teacher and loyal mentor. He's the driving force, the love and the light. He's my greatest adviser and fills me with courage and confidence. I feel terribly vulnerable without him, but I am determined not to let anyone down.

As I finish unpacking, the first student arrives. She greets me in a matter-of-fact way, as though Morgan, the greatest influence in my 40 years of living, has not died. I don't know how to react. I go along with the charade. She kindly helps me put out the chairs and then others begin arriving.

How am I going to do this? *I question myself.*

Once the tables and chairs are all arranged and everyone has a hot drink, I invite them to sit down. I start by welcoming them and then go on to share that today may be very difficult for me. My voice already begins to waver and I have to stop talking to gather myself. Everything feels so painful without Morgan.

'Don't worry, I've come equipped,' I joke, pointing to two boxes of tissues on a nearby table. 'I have a box of tissues for all of you and another box for myself!'

Laughter ripples through the room.

'Today may be a living example of power animals at work,' I explain. 'I really need the support of my animal friends today and I've brought many of them with me.'

I refer to the photos of dogs, cats and Casper the lion which are propped up on my desk as energetic links to their true essence. I also have a photo of Morgan, but I don't think he will be making an appearance; he is settling into his non-physical energetic form.

Over the course of the day the students are kind and gentle, and I am totally blown away by the animals. They demonstrate the support, guidance and courage they can give as empowering 'power' animals.

As there are five students instead of the full six, I realize I will have to partner someone during each exercise. I wonder whether Morgan had a hand in this. By partnering I will be forced to receive empowering advice, leaving no time to get reflective or emotional about my loss.

There is an exercise in my workshop which involves gifts. I've requested everyone bring a gift for another student, something personal but inexpensive. Normally I would ask an animal to choose the student or I'd ask spirit to tell me who to partner up, or sometimes I'd ask Morgan for help, but for this exercise I intuitively feel I have to offer up a visual choice. Taking six squares of paper, I write down three pairs of numbers and let everyone pick one. I have the last piece and partner a student called Cathy. I give her a gift of a feather from Lucy, a very opinionated goose and excellent animal communication teacher. Cathy has brought her gift down from Newcastle upon Tyne inside a Tupperware box cushioned with cotton wool. She presents me with a yellow rose whose petals are a gentle pink on the inside. My heart bursts open with warmth.

'I wondered if someone would bring me a rose today,' I tell her, smiling and thankful.

'There's a story behind this rose,' she says. 'When you asked us all to bring a gift of special significance I couldn't think what to choose. Later I was doing some agonizing muscle-stretching on the floor and not thinking about it at all when the inspiration to bring a bud came to me. On reflection, I can't really say where it came from, but I felt it might be from Max, our dog in spirit. I asked my partner, Ali, if it was OK with her to bring it, and she told me she had known it would be coming and had been watching it for just over a week because of some "inner knowing" which she also felt was Max. The rose also appeared to collaborate, because even though it had been awful weather that week, wet and windy and not what roses like at all, it was blooming beautifully. Ali gave me one bud in perfect condition. On the journey down I felt that it would somehow go to you rather than another student. I just didn't know how.'

Cathy's gift feels like another little 'hello from heaven' and is a huge comfort.

In the next exercise I am paired with a student called Amanda, who is linking in with Casper.

I ask, 'Who is Morgan sending to me?'

Casper shows Amanda an image. 'I can see a black dog, Pea,' she tells me. 'It's a colour picture, but blurred shape. A black dog is coming to you.'

It's the image I received earlier: a black dog of indiscernible breed.

'I think Morgan may have joined with Casper to give me that impression,' Amanda confides.

I haven't mentioned the black dog to anyone, but Amanda has received an image that resonates with my own. This is the second sign of the black dog.

9 August

Jo has kindly brought me to Glastonbury today to visit my shamanic healer. She asked me what I wanted to do and I felt Glastonbury calling me.

I am losing my physical form, losing my grounding, and I recognize I need some outside help. I feel as though I am disintegrating and parts of my energy are spreading far and wide. I guess many might describe this feeling as 'falling apart'.

All I share with the shaman is that Morgan has ascended and that I wish to feel stronger – nothing more. At the end of a powerful session one of the first things he says to me is, 'Are you aware of a black dog? Are you working with a black dog?'

I stifle a laugh and then, smiling, say, 'That's interesting. Very soon after Morgan ascended he showed me an image of a black dog faraway. Then yesterday one of my students told me a black dog was coming to me.'

'I feel the black dog is already here with you,' the shaman asserts. 'His presence is large. He comes across as stocky and stubborn.'

'Morgan was stocky and stubborn,' I observe. 'I like stubborn dogs.'

The shaman says, 'I feel he's part of the same soul group as Morgan. I see Morgan as this very large and powerful gold light over you and your heart area and the black dog feels connected to Morgan.'

It is wonderful to hear that Morgan is close and a large gold presence over me. This is also further confirmation that a black dog is on his way. This is the third sign of the black dog.

While I am having my healing session Jo goes for a wander around the shops. Once I'm out of the session she tells me, 'I've got something for you.'

I have to wait until we're at our hotel to find out what it is.

'I saw the spine on the shelf,' she says. 'I pulled it out and looked at the back cover and then flipped through the pages and changed my mind and felt it wasn't for you, but when I turned it over to look at the front cover I couldn't believe it.'

She hands me the book. I look at the front cover and into the gentle wise eyes of a dog looking to the right in the way that Morgan would often look. I have a photo of him in the same pose. The ears of the dog are shaped just like Morgan's and look just as soft, but I'm looking at a pure black dog. And it's a book that's saying it's all right to grieve when an animal dies.

This is the fourth sign.

Chapter 13

Morgan: Beagles, Black Dogs and the Ashes

14 August 2011

I finally feel able to voice to Jo how I felt when we disagreed over Morgan's transition.

She explains that her biggest concern was that I was misreading or mishearing his communication and not accepting his desire to ascend. She felt he was suffering and it was time to assist his transition.

I do believe some people find it so hard to face death they go into denial and animals are held here longer than they wish. That's why I regularly questioned Morgan on whether he was ready to ascend. Now I feel that, too often, he was continually asked, 'Are you ready to go?' Even then, I got to the point where I thought he might feel I was trying to get rid of him by checking on such a regular basis, so I made it clear I wished to be sure he knew it was his decision and that I loved every moment we were together.

I knew through communication he was struggling but very much wanted to continue and still valued living. Part of me did question, Doesn't Jo trust me to do the right thing? Maybe she doesn't believe in what I do after all?

Now she is able to explain that when she began spending more time at home, rather than just a snatched day or two here or there between jobs, she was able to tell how much Morgan loved life and was battling to enjoy every moment.

She asks, 'Can you forgive me?'

Glancing over to Morgan's photo, I hear him tell me, 'Forgive her.'

Before she leaves to catch a train to Cardiff, I let her know it's now in the past and I remind myself that we're both learning from Morgan's teachings.

We're both on the Morgan train to enlightenment!

15 August

I write to Lynne and explain Morgan has given me an image of the new dog he is sending.

She replies, 'It's really odd that you should mention your new dog today. Morgan came through this morning and asked me to tell you to get ready for his apprentice, so I suspected that there was some animal in the pipeline. I think you just need to be on the watch for hints and clues.'

At 4:32 p.m. I feel the urge to look at the Mayhew Animal Home website. I am drawn to a link that will explain the adoption process 'by clicking here'. Having gone through the process with Morgan, I don't need to click, but something guides me to anyway. The image of a large black dog fills the screen; he is a German shepherd with an open, happy, intelligent face. Beneath his picture are the words: 'At the Mayhew Animal Home we believe in finding the right dog for the right owner.'

Beyond doubt Morgan is confirming there is a black dog coming to me. A rescue dog. The right dog.

This is the fifth sign of the black dog.

16 August

Someone asks me, 'Will you get another dog?'

I feel taken aback. It's less than four weeks since Morgan transitioned. If my loss had been my father, would they have asked, 'Are you going to get another father?' Or comment, 'You can always get another one,' if my mother had just died? Morgan has been family to me.

I motivate myself to do something positive – I watch The Lion King *on DVD and it leaves me feeling uplifted.*

Tonight I dream of Morgan. I am with him and he is with me in such a real way that I am able to stroke the hair along his back and feel it completely. In fact it doesn't feel like a dream. I can see his eyes and we are here together in a blissful moment of reunion. Maybe he has come to me or I have gone to him, but it doesn't matter because I am with him and touching his body and stroking his hair is so real, as real as it was before his death. This is the best dream experience I have ever had and my heart is bursting with immeasurable joy.

17 August

Jo is now working at the Edinburgh Festival. It's the first time she's been away from home since Morgan transitioned and she found it hard to leave.

The creative team is in typical Edinburgh Festival accommodation: a large flat with five or six bedrooms. Jo and the set designer, lovely Tom, are first to arrive and have the pick of the rooms. Jo rings me in the evening to explain what happened.

As they looked around, she found herself walking into a large bedroom. The first thing that struck her was an enormous painting over the bed, which showed a French café front with tables but no people. But who should be standing at the café doorway? A black dog.

She explains, 'He was a large dog and I think he was supposed to be a Labrador but because of the crude style of the painting his legs were just a bit too long and his body slim and not solid enough. Even the ears were wrong. He was a funny-looking thing, but I knew instantly that this was going to be my room and I was going to sleep below the black dog, who was looking out for me.'

When she showed Tom the painting and explained, as a dog-lover himself, he immediately agreed she could take that room.

It is the sixth sign of the black dog.

18 August

Tonight I have arranged to visit friends, Belinda and Laura and their delightful cats, Gypsy, Max, Beau and Herbert-George. I am missing Morgan badly and wonder about cancelling, but as I look at his photo on the mantelpiece I hear him tell me, 'It will be good for you.' So I get in the car and despite the torrential rain make my way over to Battersea.

My friends are kind and gentle and don't ask questions. They allow me to just be. When I first walk into their kitchen, I notice straightaway a beautiful single pink rose. Over time I feel more relaxed and able to share with them some of the wonderful moments I'm experiencing with the black dog and pink roses.

When I get home I receive a text message from Laura with a photo of their pink rose:

'Did you happen to notice this on our kitchen worktop tonight? Been there over a week. I didn't have the heart to throw it out.'

Now we know why.

19 August

Jo is still away, but she has sent me a stunning rose bush – pink, of course. I was thinking about planting a pink rose for Morgan only yesterday.

The doorbell rings a second time and I unwrap a framed certificate stating that a star has been named in honour of Morgan in the constellation Canis Major. He'd be pleased it was Canis Major and not Canis Minor, because although a small-sized dog, he always identified with the larger breeds. My thoughtful friend Sandra D. has named the star Morgan master teacher canine friend. *Perfect.*

20 August

I am teaching Stage 2 of my 'Empowering Animals' course. At the end of the workshop my student friend Amanda and I head to Morgan's pub. Immediately inside the door I come face to face with a gigantic pure black long-haired German shepherd identical to the one on the Mayhew Animal Home website. His name is Woofie, he's a gentle giant and he tells me he doesn't mind his name. A pure black Lab passes me. Then outside there is a pure black Staffie with a slightly grey muzzle sitting beside two older men with pints of beer. Three black dog signs within just a few minutes: seven, eight and nine.

The Staffie greets us enthusiastically. I fuss him and his guardian says to me, 'Would you get one? There are lots at Battersea Dogs' and Cats' Home.'

For a moment I am speechless, rooted to the spot, looking the man in the eyes. After a pause to compose myself, I manage to voice calmly, 'My dog died three weeks ago. He was from the Mayhew Animal Home.'

There is silence for a moment. But then the man offers words of sincere sympathy and I can see empathy is his eyes.

'I think it's too soon just now,' I say. 'When I do feel ready I will pick a mutt, a crossbreed.'

'You'll pick the right one,' he says.

I smile and nod.

As we walk away, Amanda repeats his sentence: 'You'll pick the right one… If only he knew how right he is!'

It felt like reassurance from Morgan that I will know the right black dog when our paths cross. There'll be no need to worry about picking the wrong one.

21 August

Grief is a bit like the sea, smooth and calm one moment, then crashing and overwhelming the next. Grief comes to me in waves.

1 September

Today becomes a breakthrough day. I manage to get myself to yoga: the first time in many months. It sounds such a meaningless thing, but really it is no small feat. I leave with a satisfying sense of accomplishment. I am moving forward and re-engaging with life. It is a baby step, maybe, but a step all the same.

Another sympathy card arrives. This one has the same image of tree trunks and bluebells that is on the biodegradable cardboard tube containing Morgan's ashes. More synchronicity.

2 September

I return the phone call of a man whose dog died just two weeks ago. I can feel his pain and how he's trying to hold it together. I ask the dog's name and immediately see an image of a black-and-white collie. Without prompting, the man confirms the image in my mind. He says he's not coping, but he is able to pick up the phone and ask for help, which is such a positive step. I talk to him and validate that his feelings are perfectly natural until he feels much better and is happy to end the call. He may contact me in the future to communicate with his dog.

Once off the phone I realize I am feeling stronger and will be able to return to work next week.

6 September

I try to wash Morgan's bed today. I place the bottom cushion into the washing machine, but that's as far as I get. I sniff the outside of the oval fleece and can still smell him. I remove the bottom cushion from the machine and return the bed to its home in my office.

13 October

'Chasing Cars' by Snow Patrol is playing. It's one of our songs. I think back to when Morgan and I would lie on the grass together. These moments were heaven for us, literally heaven on Earth. We would lie there gazing into each other's eyes and just forget the world. There was such a knowing and such a depth of love. I felt bathed in his grace.

1 November

Today I feel peace. The distress I have felt over Morgan's physical absence is feeling bearable and I welcome it. As soon as time moved to 1/11/11 there was a shift. A numerologist would probably have something to say about this.

I feel I now have a sense of harmony and understanding. I no longer feel as though I am falling through the cracks. I have a deep acceptance of Morgan's transition from physical form and I am encompassed by a feeling of unconditional love – Morgan's love.

8 December

After much consideration I feel able to scatter Morgan's ashes tomorrow. I have asked Morgan about it and he's told me, 'It will be good for you – both of you.'

Jo has been keen to scatter his ashes before the end of the year so 2012 can be 'a fresh start'.

'Would you like us to scatter them tomorrow?' I asked Morgan.

'Yes,' he answered agreeably.

Nearly five months after his body was cremated I've reached a place where I can release his remains back to the Earth. I have moved into acceptance and feel able to let go.

9 December

The sun is full and bright and the sky is pale winter blue. Winter has arrived late, so the trees are still beautifully dressed in their autumnal shades of toffee, coffee and chocolate. We're returning to the place where we had the most fun together, the place where Morgan ran with joy, a big beaming smile and twinkling eyes of pure happiness. We're back at his common.

His ashes are still in the recycling tube with the forest design of trees and bluebells. We carry the cylinder in a day pack along with a flask of coffee, a garden fork and a heart-shaped seeded memorial to plant, which, if we're lucky, will produce forget-me-nots in spring.

As we exit the car park, the first dog that crosses our path is a beagle. We begin by going for a walk along one of the routes we enjoyed together, remembering moments of Morgan's earlier life when he kept us on the hop. We pass many golfers and numerous people out walking their dogs. The weather is beautiful, so this isn't unexpected.

About 30 minutes later we reach the special tree. Ever since his stroke we've known this will be where we'll scatter Morgan's ashes. He has asked us to scatter them here and we agree this is 'the special place'.

Jo gives the tree a hug, a kiss and, unbeknown to me, says silently, 'Look after him.'

Round the other side, I touch the tree, express a feeling of love and gratitude and request, 'Please look after him.'

The response comes, 'I will look after him.'

This has always been a maternal tree to me – a tree with a strong feminine energy that is both loving and protective.

We take our time. We sit for a moment on the tree roots while we wait for golfers to pass. Then there is silence, so we take out the tube. Jo takes my hand and begins to scatter Morgan's ashes. Shafts of sunlight illuminate the deep green grass to our side. Independently, we've both thought it would be nice to release the ashes around the tree in a circle and then in pockets within the tree trunk.

We take it in turns to scatter the ashes, which are white and grit-like. The ground is blanketed in the first of the autumn leaves and the ashes fall over them, leaving a dusting that looks like light snow.

Once we've both circled the tree, we put the remaining ashes in nooks and crannies of the trunk. We then take some long fallen twigs and gently brush the leaves so the ashes can fall through to the earth below.

The sun continues to shine, the birds are quiet and for the entire time it takes us to do this the vicinity of the tree and the surrounding areas, from which we can be viewed, remain completely empty. It is as though for these 10 minutes or so we are in our own vacuum of time, in a silent and sacred space. The golfers, joggers, walkers and dogs have just vanished. It is just the two of us, the Mother tree and our dear Morgan.

Once we've finished, we put the empty tube back into the day pack and within seconds a black dog runs up to us. Then a few seconds later there is another pure black dog, and then a minute after that another black dog: three black dogs, one after the other in quick succession. Signs 10, 11 and 12.

Immediately golfers appear, followed by more dog-walkers with different-coloured dogs. We take out our flask, sit on the tree roots again and drink coffee while watching golf balls flying past *as we're acknowledged by dog after dog after dog, all complete strangers to us. We plant the heart-shaped forget-me-not seeds, pat down the soil and then decide to walk back.*

Approaching the car park, our eyes are drawn to a car. A dog is inside it, waiting for his guardian. When we get closer, we can see he is another beagle.

Morgan's beagle presence greeted us as we arrived. Three black dogs greeted us, one straight after the other, immediately after scattering his ashes. Then, before we left, another beagle said goodbye.

Part V
MESSAGES FROM BEYOND THE GRAVE

'The most beautiful things in the world cannot be seen or even touched. They must be felt with the heart.'
HELEN KELLER

Chapter 14
Forever Loyal Barni Bear

❦

*'The soul is learning by experience. The mind limits the
experience, but the heart knows. Listen to the heart
more. This is where the truth resides – in the feelings.'*
BARNI

What happens if your animal goes missing and you're not
able to say goodbye? How do you find peace in order
to move forward? In this chapter Barni shares his view on the
purpose of loss and explains what it is like in the afterlife.

Barni's guardian, Jacqui, was a middle-aged mental health
professional with a big love of felines. She had contacted me
because her seven-year-old cat, Barni, had gone missing.
Previously, Barni had vanished for 10 days and returned thin and
frightened. This time he'd disappeared just before Jacqui had
gone away on holiday and still hadn't reappeared when she'd got
back two weeks later.

A photogenic Norwegian Forest cat looked up at me from
a recumbent position in the photograph I was holding. I was
immediately struck by the intensity of the large golden eyes
looking directly down the camera lens. With his head to the
right, his hips to the left and his long-haired tail wrapped
round the front of his body, Barni was an impressive sight.

The second thing that struck me was the pale grey Elizabethan ruff framing his strong lion-like face and large bold ears. Barni was a cat of notable handsomeness, with marbles of glorious grey fur progressing throughout his body, accenting his regal pale heart-shaped ruff and the darker stripes working outwards across his back in perfect parallels. Shades of grey had never been more enchanting.

Jacqui wrote:

'We chose Barni after losing our beautiful Maine Coon, Jasper, to kidney cancer... Norwegian Forest cats look a bit similar to Maine Coons and are big cats but generally easy-going and friendly. I came across a woman through the Norwegian Forest Cat Club whose surname was "Healing", which appealed to me. She sent me pictures of her litter and I chose Barni, who was known then as Barni Rubble. When he was 12 weeks old my six-year-old daughter, Jess, and I were able to go and collect him. After considerable discussion on the trip home we finally settled on calling him Barni, but to me he will always be my Barni Bear.'

It was one of England's well-known blue-grey days when I first sat in my office to forge a connection with Barni. I was immediately struck by his wisdom. He came across as a wise soul with a mature and regal air. He also had a measured, even temperament. He didn't have a mean bone in his body. To see whether we had a good connection, I began by asking him when he'd gone missing. He gave me the impression it was late afternoon and Jacqui confirmed that.

I got the sense Barni loved climbing trees and had a courageous and adventurous nature. He showed me he was very agile and found jumping effortless. In further imagery he pictured sunbathing in front of floor-to-ceiling glass and being given a special diet in the form of prescription dry biscuits. He expressed happiness as he pictured himself batting at water from the tap, catching butterflies and hunting mice. Jacqui confirmed these details and also the impressions I'd received that Barni was neutered, micro-chipped and didn't wear a collar.

'We used to put a collar and ID tag on him but he came home on numerous occasions without them, so we just gave up in the end.'

Barni went on to reveal that he'd been missing his feline friend, Sacha, who'd been killed in a car accident. I felt they used to be very close and he'd been unable to accept that he was no longer with him. Jacqui said she felt the same.

Barni shared a random image of a small spaniel or Jack Russell-sized dog who was quite noisy and bouncy.

'We have a small King Charles spaniel who is full of life,' Jacqui said. 'He could be the small, noisy, bouncy dog.'

Barni then showed a very sweet image where he was draping his paws round Jacqui's neck and giving her a 'hug'.

'Barni is the gentlest creature,' she told me. 'The way he puts his huge soft velvety paws onto either side of my face and literally pulls my face around to look directly into his eyes is not something I ever remember another pet doing. And at other times he just puts a paw either side of my neck and relaxes.'

I got the sense that Barni had gone because he wasn't coping without Sacha. I could feel he was sad and grieving. I felt he was still in his physical body and he gave me the impression he would like to go home.

When I asked him where he was, he showed me the route he had taken. He had gone out of the garden and to the right on what felt like his normal patrol route and had had to stay high off the ground because there were dogs to the right and he couldn't cut through their garden. Continuing in that direction, he pictured a copse or larger wooded area that he liked to visit. He gave images of going under a very large gate and across a field to this copse. On the other side of it he pictured another field and an orderly housing estate. There was a woman in that direction who fed him.

Jacqui said the information made perfect sense. She didn't know if any of her neighbours were feeding Barni, but said she wouldn't put it past them, as he was a real charmer.

The final image from Barni was of something that looked a bit like a propeller, but I felt I was looking at it the wrong way up.

Jacqui later got back to me with further information:

> 'When Barni went missing on a previous occasion my neighbour told me that a nearby farmer had once arrived on her doorstep with him, asking if he was her cat. She had told him where I lived, but he didn't turn up and sadly I didn't know anything about this at the time. Thankfully, Barni did return that time. You mentioned a particular object like a propeller that was upside down. I found this object on the land owned by the man my neighbour had mentioned. It is some kind of air-pollution measuring device. I asked at the farm, but they denied having seen Barni and even denied talking to my neighbour on the previous occasion he went missing. This didn't seem right and made me feel uncomfortable.'

Jacqui continued to ask people about Barni and ensured her missing cat posters remained up, but sadly we were unable to locate him. Still, she remained optimistic:

> 'Jess and I both have dreams that he is home or coming home and we take these as good signs.'

It was April the following year when Jacqui made contact again.

'I had a strong sense of urgency to call you,' she wrote. 'I feel that Barni wants me or is lost or ill, maybe unable to find his way home.'

Some time between her e-mail and the time I was able to reach her, due to my prior client commitments, she'd had an even more urgent feeling Barni needed to connect. When I communicated with him, I could sense he was a very still and powerful presence. I also felt he had ascended.

'More peacefully than you will ever know,' he told me. 'She knows I have ascended too.'

It seemed to me that Barni had been put to sleep. To be sure this information was from him, though, I went through some new impressions with Jacqui. In one image he showed that he loved being brushed while on a lap.

'Oh, yes – say "brush" to him and he'd come running,' Jacqui verified.

Barni showed he liked to follow Jacqui round the garden. He came across as more like a dog than a cat, but he did love to climb trees, which dogs still have to master! He expressed a sense that he and Jacqui had a very close heart connection. Once Jacqui had confirmed these and other details, I had the unenviable task of sensitively sharing with her my impression that Barni had now transitioned from his body.

'I knew you were going to say that to me,' she said. 'In my heart, I already knew he had died.' Nevertheless, in the hope that her gut feeling was wrong and Barni was still alive, she went on, 'Can he give us any clues so that we can find him?'

'Not in this lifetime,' Barni replied. 'You have to let me go now.'

'Does he know that we love and miss him and think about him often?'

'I feel it in my heart every day. We were special. I will never forget that.'

'Does he know he has left a huge gap, especially in my life, and that I will never forget him?'

'Yes, but I am still with you, more subtly than before, but still with you. You miss my physical presence, my character, but I am still with you, lying on your bed and watching you in the garden. Forever loyal.'

Some people don't think of cats as a loyal species, but I have communicated with cats who have expressed incredible faithfulness to their guardians. You only have to take a read of *A Street Cat Named Bob* by James Bowen to see an example of how an incredibly loyal cat helped turn a man's life around.

'Does Barni have any message for us or the other animals?' Jacqui asked me.

'Be still and quiet, my love, and you will sense me, feel me, see me, hear me. I am all around you and within you. Energetically, we are One.'

At the end Jacqui said, 'I have experienced a lot of loss in my life. Jasper and two other much-loved cats were lost to cancer, three other cats were lost to car accidents, and our second Sacha, Sacha 2, and Barni vanished at a time when there were a lot of pet thefts in the area. Having had so many major losses, I have to ask: is there a purpose to all this?'

Barni answered, 'The purpose of loss is always the same: growth – growth of the soul to divine awareness. The pain is part of letting go because the soul has not comprehended that life goes on. The soul is learning by experience. The mind limits the experience, but the heart knows. Listen to the heart more. This is where the truth resides – in the feelings.'

Despite the pain of letting go, Jacqui was glad to hear from Barni and later revealed:

'*After the communication there was a sense of relief and release that he could now be at peace. Although I was not able to say goodbye in person, I do feel our communication helped enormously. When he communicated that his death was "more peaceful than I could ever know" and we both felt he may have been put to sleep, I felt reassured that someone had had the compassion to help him and take him to a vet.*

Not being able to have a ceremony for him in our garden was very difficult. Barni was a huge part of my life, and still is. I still grieve for him and I don't think I have fully found peace within myself. At some point we need to have some sort of memorial for him. However, as I say this, I feel he is telling me he is fully alive and just fine, thank you. No memorial needed! He is still very alive for me in many ways. Sometimes when I feel his presence laughter comes.

I can see that Barni was helping me on my soul journey; he helped me on my journey of learning to be. I have always had a strong connection with animals and I feel I've been able to have a calming effect on them. It is as though they feel understood. Having such a strong connection with animals has enabled me to believe in myself a bit more too.

I now believe that those we love are not lost to us. We may not have that physical connection with them but they are with us in our hearts and minds.'

Another form of reassurance came from the way Barni finished his communication. He expressed a great sense of peace as he explained what it felt like to experience the afterlife: 'It is as though I am floating, as air, as aether, free and limitless.'

In the next chapter you'll read about Boo Boo, a budgerigar who died very quickly from an accident but taught his guardian how to heal her broken heart when he communicated in his new spirit form.

Chapter 15
Boo Boo Budgerigar

⟨◦⟩

'Believe in people's goodness to attract that to you.'
BOO BOO

Boo Boo passed over on 6 May 2009, aged 12 and a half. His guardian, Roz, was a tall woman, aged 45 and living in London. She'd not been able to say goodbye because Boo Boo's death had been sudden and tragic. It had been an accident, but Roz felt responsible and sick with guilt, which was consuming her day by day.

Roz's decision to share her life with another sentient being had not been an easy one. It had meant the end of her days in rehab for one eating disorder or another, one addiction or another. 'It was time to grow up and take responsibility, not only for myself, but for another being,' she admitted.

As a child, she had had budgerigars as family pets, so she knew they were special little birds, but nothing had prepared her for the uniqueness of Boo.

She had set her heart on a blue male budgie and had been reassured by the breeder she approached that he had all colours, but disappointment struck when she arrived because there were no blue budgies. Instead the breeder showed her two dominant pied brothers. He put both birds into a show cage and when Roz put her finger through the bars, the one she considered bolder but less beautiful walked over and held the tip of it with his foot.

'It was as if he'd chosen me,' she shared. 'I knew I would always regret it if I didn't take him home.'

Roz and Boo became inseparable. They shared meals from the same plate; Boo loved vegetables, fruit, wholegrain rice and toast. Between mouthfuls he would stretch his earnest little face towards Roz for a quick kiss and cuddle.

From the age of one he began to learn a huge vocabulary and eventually made up his own sentences, always getting nouns and verbs in the right place: 'Who's my boy? Are you a *deeeear* little munchkin? I *love* you. Are you OK? *Heeeeeello!* Wicky, wicky, wild, wild *pest!* You're a *beeeeautiful* little bird, aren't you? *Baby* Boo! You're a *special* Boo! Aren't you *gorgeous!* What a *cute* little sausage!'

When Roz needed Boo to go inside his cage she just said 'Innn you pop!' and he would 'run' – move at a high-speed waddle – across the cage top, abseil down the bars to his outdoor perch and hop inside, pulling the door shut as he went.

Boo spent a lot of time on the top of his cage playing with various balls, bells and weighted toys that hit him back on the beak if he attacked them. He thought it hilarious to throw all these toys off and get Roz to pick them all up again. He also had a thing about red biros and liked chasing the writing, and his idea of bliss was to roll around in a huge bunch of wet parsley until he was totally soaked.

Trust blossomed between him and his guardian, and Roz used to get her face preened, even her eyelashes. Boo would often press his head under her nose or climb onto her shoulder, where he'd snuggle into her neck and fall asleep. He could be just as gentle with strangers, but if he felt uneasy he'd go back inside his cage and pull the door shut behind him. Then, when he felt safe enough, he'd come out and reintroduce himself.

Roz went back to college to study garden design, which led to her becoming a professional garden designer and two years later a part-time teacher at the college while continuing her garden business the rest of the time. Boo accepted everything without complaint and always gave her a head-bobbing welcome home, accompanied by taps on her nose and lips with his beak.

In April 2004 they moved house and soon after Boo became ill. Roz felt the stress of the move had weakened his immune system.

'I was very worried, since birds only show symptoms of illness if they are very sick. It was a Sunday and we'd never needed a vet. I got him an emergency veterinary appointment; however, it turned out the vet knew very little about birds. Boo was given an antibiotic shot and I was given contact numbers for the only two avian vets in London. The next day one of these vets diagnosed Boo with psittacosis.'

Psittacosis, also known as parrot fever, is a disease caused by the bacteria *Chlamydia psittaci*.

'I thought I was going to lose him,' Roz said, 'but he did recover. However, he was never 100 per cent after that.'

Boo began to get arthritis and found it increasingly difficult to fly. He began to leap off his cage onto the hard floor for no apparent reason. Roz felt the new house had strange creaks and crackles, which unsettled him. After one episode she noticed his ankle was swelling. It was the start of gout and so Boo's leg ring had to be removed before it became uncomfortable. An X-ray showed his bones were very thin and mottled.

'I didn't know he should have been having calcium and vitamin D supplements due to lack of natural sunlight,' Roz shared.

Roz surrounded Boo's cage with bath mats and rugs, but on the odd occasion he would throw himself further than expected and miss them. This resulted in a fracture to one wing and another fracture to the hip. By now Boo was receiving daily medication for gout, and painkillers too. Medication soon became twice daily, but he was always very good and would jump onto Roz's hand when she asked him and allow her to syringe them into his mouth.

Kobe, the Blue-Headed Pionus

Roz decided to add to her avian family. She found a four-month-old blue-headed Pionus parrot right at the end of the breeding season and, just after Boo's eleventh birthday, he came into their lives.

> *'Kobe loved Boo from the moment his zygodactyly clawed feet arrived in his new home and he'd copy everything Boo did: when Boo preened, Kobe preened; when Boo ate, Kobe ate. Boo even taught Kobe to say "Hello!" But Kobe's arrival was not all good news. He was a playful baby and would sometimes fly too close to Boo and startle him into jumping off his cage.'*

Roz tried to encourage Boo to stay inside, but he wanted to be out on top of his cage as he'd always been. He even had a budgie tantrum if Roz kept the cage door shut: he'd climb using his good foot and beak and vocalize until she opened it.

Due to his gout, Boo couldn't abseil any more, and he couldn't climb down the spiral rope perch alternative, so if Roz wasn't there and he wanted to go in, he'd leap. Roz piled up more bath mats and when she was there she began to predict when he'd leap and run to catch him.

One night about 10 o'clock Boo was in a rush to enter his cage. Roz saw him preparing to jump and just managed to catch him in time. However, the relief was short-lived. Kobe wanted to see what all the commotion was about and appeared out of nowhere. He landed on Roz's wrist and Boo went tumbling out of her hands onto a hard stone part of the floor.

'How I pleaded for time to reverse just a few seconds, but it didn't. Boo lay on the floor with his leg broken. I gently picked him up and placed him in a homemade hospital cage with bubble wrap and towels. The vets were shut, so I couldn't get him help until the next morning. All I could do was give him painkillers and his favourite toy bell. It was the worst and longest night of our lives. As soon as the vet opened, I took Boo in, leaving Kobe covered and still sleeping.

The rush-hour traffic was horrendous that morning and it doubled the normal journey. Tears streamed down my face the whole way. Boo lay on his hospital cage in the passenger seat, trying to play with his bell.

When we arrived we had to wait our turn in the waiting room. When the vet came to us he was cross because I hadn't given Boo any painkillers that morning. I was too upset to say I hadn't known whether to or not, as I had been concerned they could counteract the anaesthetic. The vet told me they'd operate later and Boo was taken out the back.

As the veterinary staff handed me his empty cage they explained that I wasn't allowed to stay with him. I left the surgery sobbing. Somehow I knew I would never see him again. It took half an hour to compose myself before I could drive home.'

Roz waited with Kobe all morning for news. Then at 12:28 p.m. the phone rang.

'We just lost him,' the voice said. 'We managed to bind his leg and he was coming round from the anaesthetic, but then it appeared as though he just gave up.'

Roz told the vet it wasn't his fault and thanked him for what he'd done. He offered to bury Boo in the park because Roz didn't have a garden, but she declined and instead agreed to have him cremated.

'My soul mate of almost 13 years had just gone. I cried and cried. Very soon the "what if", "if only" and "I shouldn't have" thoughts began to race through my mind. What if I'd given him painkillers that morning? If only I hadn't dropped him... I shouldn't have got Kobe.

My world was empty without Boo. I felt totally lost. The guilt was crippling and I didn't go into work for the rest of the week.'

Boo Boo's Consultation

Roz came across my book and after locating my website e-mailed a list of questions and messages for Boo.

'I never said goodbye to him,' she wrote. 'There is still so much left unsaid and I feel so guilty. More than anything, I want to tell him how sorry I feel.'

I don't receive as many bird clients as dogs, cats and horses, so I always delight in being able to communicate with a winged species. I first met Boo a year after his transition, during one of the coolest August months in 17 years. London was cloaked in grey clouds and heavy rain was causing flash floods across many parts of the UK. In his photo, however, Boo was looking very bright. Turquoise is one of my favourite colours and he wore it to great effect. He was pictured in profile from his chest up. He had white feathers on his crown and white plumage defined by black barring, giving the impression of zebra stripes, across the top of his head, down the nape of his neck and at the front by his throat. Mingled in with the stripes were flecks of turquoise and a vivid royal blue cheek patch. His beak was greenish-yellow and the cere, the area above containing the nostrils, was turquoise, indicating this was a cock budgie, not a hen.

Straightaway I felt that Boo was a special soul with a sage side to his character. I felt this wasn't his first flight – he had reincarnated. Moving on from his wiser nature, I then felt the complete opposite: Boo was quite opinionated, especially about humans! However, I sensed he was very sweet to Roz and liked a lot of physical contact with her. I realized he was her wise teacher.

Further communication revealed that Boo liked to knock a bell, he enjoyed a lot of freedom and there was another bird of similar size to him whose company he didn't much welcome. He also showed something orange in colour. The relationship between Boo and Roz seemed based on equality, and if Roz called out to him, he would call back.

I ran these first impressions by Roz, who came back with confirmation. The orange thing turned out to be an orange paddle in his bath that he liked to turn to get drops of water to drink. In fact he would only drink this way. But Roz wasn't surprised he'd mentioned his bell first:

'He adored his special bell. It was a round "cat" mesh ball with a bell inside and another bell I had attached to the bottom. One day I got home to find him very quiet and sad. Then I noticed his bell lying broken on the floor of his cage. I mended it and hung it up again and he was absolutely ecstatic. He always had to have that bell near him and usually held onto it with one foot when inside his cage.'

Content it was a good connection, Roz and I arranged a phone appointment to go through Boo's communication.

Her first question was: 'Are you happy now?'

Boo's reply was honest and to the point. 'I would be happier with you. Soul mates. You truly understood me.'

I added, 'I am feeling Boo could be complex – he didn't always follow the rules.'

Roz readily agreed and then asked him, 'How do you feel physically?'

'Free and light,' Boo replied, 'the lightest I have ever felt. It is a joyous feeling.'

I guess it was an odd question, because Boo didn't have a body now, but it was interesting to hear how a soul feels when existing as pure energy without form.

Roz went very quiet when I read out her next message for Boo: 'I miss you and I love you.'

'I know. I feel it. We have a strong bond,' he replied.

Next came the reason Roz had sought the communication in the first place: '*I'm sorry I let you down.*'

'Don't ever think that,' was Boo's lightning-fast response. 'We are in this together. Forever and ever. Pals.'

Roz was quiet. I wondered if she could absorb what Boo was communicating. I continued gently and read her next message: 'I'm sorry you were in so much pain.'

'Pain is manageable,' Boo replied, 'more manageable than you'll believe. One day you will understand the strength in being light and free – flying is a blessing in many ways.'

Then Roz asked, 'Are you still with me?'

'On and off. Mostly I am busy elsewhere. You know I cannot stay around long. I check on you and feel your heart is sad and lonely.'

'Will you reincarnate?' she asked, adding, 'I know it's probably futile, but I'm hoping that he might choose to reincarnate and we can be together again.'

'Not now. I am too happy here. Find yourself a new soul mate on Earth,' Boo replied, but not in a malicious way.

'Would you like to see me again? And, if so, how can I find you?'

'You can reach me in your dreams. This is the best place for now. You still have a lot of living to do. Talk to me in your sleep.'

Animals often tell me it is easier to reach the humans they love in their sleep because they are in an altered state of consciousness that enables the connection. Sometimes the velocity of a guardian's grief blocks the animal from reaching them. A desperate desire to hear from the animal can also inhibit the connection. So, if you want an animal to reach you, relaxing and letting go of your desperate need can be the most effective way of allowing it to happen.

We had now arrived at Roz's final question: 'Is there anything you would like to say to me?'

'Yes – keep your heart open now. Believe in people's goodness to attract that to you. Stop sleeping on the wrong side of the bed – move over to the other side. Bring lightness into your being.'

Down the phone line I could hear Roz fighting back the tears, but I was unaware of her physical movements when I described what Boo was picturing to me: 'He's showing me that he's lying on your heart chakra and looking straight into your eyes.'

Roz was stunned and speechless. She didn't let on until the next day, when she sent an explanation:

'Moments before you said that Boo was lying on my heart I had put my curled hand there as if I was holding something... it must have been Boo. And there's another thing: Boo had always slept next to my bed and I had always slept as near as I could to him. Even when he'd gone, I still slept on that side of the bed. I felt "Stop sleeping on the wrong side of the bed – move over to the other side" was his way of telling me it was time to move on.

*I had no expectations about the communication; I just
knew it was something I had to do. What surprised me was
that the information you gave was so personal to Boo that
it couldn't have been about any other bird. You had me
fighting back the tears all through.'*

Ollie, the Orange-winged Amazon

By the time Roz received her communication with Boo she'd
already introduced a new bird to the family. Ollie was an orange-
winged Amazon. Around 13 inches long, he was mainly a green
parrot with blue and yellow head feathers and vivid orange flashes
in his wings and tail. Roz hadn't purposefully gone looking for
another bird, but a set of circumstances had led to Ollie flying
straight into her life.

Roz had read about his plight on a parrot forum. The woman
who'd rescued him was trying to rehome him because 'he wasn't
coming on as she expected', but nobody was interested.

*'I thought if people knew what was wrong with him he'd
have more of a chance of finding a new home, so I offered
to pay for him to see an avian vet. Then, since I'd paid,
it was assumed that I was interested in him. I was, but I
thought it would be too much work. Still, something else
kept saying, "You'll always regret it if you don't – it's time
to stop playing safe!"'*

Ollie was a bigger bird than Roz was used to and he wasn't tame.
He'd been badly neglected and by the time he was rescued, he
was very ill. An endoscopy revealed he had *Aspergillosis*, a fungal
disease that affects the respiratory system. Due to his sunflower-
seed diet, he was badly vitamin A deficient, and due to neglect he
also had a weakened immune system. These factors led to him
suffering from inflamed mucus membranes. His nares were also

swollen and blocked, his eyes were covered in bubbles of mucus, he had difficulty breathing, his claws were terribly overgrown and one had grown full circle and was digging back into his foot. He obviously needed some care and attention. And Boo knew that Roz had needs too. In a second communication he informed her, 'I gave Ollie to you. You need something wild in your life.'

Sometimes animals are sent to us, sometimes they choose to be with us to help us heal or grow and sometimes they know we need them just as much as they need us. As Roz commented:

'It does feel that Ollie belongs to us. Boo always had a great sense of humour. I am always aware that he described me as a bird in a cage and he wants me to be freer. It is hard to do physically, as I hate leaving Kobe and Ollie for longer than I have to, but mentally I believe I am becoming freer.

Each of the three birds has contributed to where I am right now. My world has expanded enormously... Boo got me living again, Kobe started me researching and learning about parrot diet and behaviour (because he was always so naughty), and Ollie furthered my behavioural knowledge and now I am researching and practising treating his illness holistically.

On this journey of learning with the birds I have met the most incredible people who have been unbelievably generous with their time and knowledge, and the most amazing opportunities have come my way, from writing articles for Parrots magazine to tutoring on the parrot behaviour online courses 'Living and Learning with Parrots' and 'Parrot (Behaviour Analysis Solutions) Mini Lessons' – both developed and originally taught by Dr Susan Friedman, a psychology professor who pioneered the application of Applied Behaviour Analysis to captive and companion animals.

Boo wants me to believe in people's goodness to attract that to myself, and now it's easier to do this because I am surrounded by it daily. I want to say "Thank you, Boo. You will always be in my heart. I love you and I'm sorry."'

Through hearing from Boo, Roz was able to dissolve her guilt and engage with positive states of being – an excitement for life, a zest for learning and a desire to empower others through her new-found knowledge of parrots. Even when things feel at the lowest point they can change and morph into positivity. Where there is loss, there can be new life; where there is guilt, there can be deeper understanding and love. Forgiveness is one of life's greatest gifts, especially when we learn to forgive ourselves.

The next chapter is about a Christian guardian who believed in life after death and wanted to make sure her cat, Milka, was OK in the afterlife.

Chapter 16
Milka, *mon Petit*

◌∽◌

*'Live a happy life. Make it happy. Don't
always rely on others to make it happy for
you. Be proud. Be proud of who you are.'*
MILKA

'I'm a Christian and I strongly believe in life after death, but I
need help to make sure Milka is fine "out there". I miss her so
much. I love her so much. She means the world to me.'

Milka died on 31 January 2010, aged 13 years and six
months. Three weeks later her guardian, Catherine, contacted
me for a communication.

Catherine was living in her home country, France, when she first
brought Milka into her life. She was 20 years old, had just started
renting her first flat, in Bayonne, and was feeling lonely. Having
shared her life with cats since she was a child, she adored them and
decided to look in the pet section of a free local newspaper for a kitten.
She answered an ad and went to meet a lady who brought out two
kittens to show her, one totally black and the other black and white.
Catherine loved black cats and had thought she would chose the
black one if there was one in the litter, but her heart was taken the
moment she laid eyes on the black-and-white kitten. She picked her
immediately, without even knowing whether she was a boy or a girl.

At first they found it hard to become friends. There was no garden and not even a balcony, so Milka spent a lot of time inside on her own while Catherine was working all day. But a move to Toulouse changed everything. Catherine went back to university and was able to spend more time at home. Milka came out of her shell and began to show a little affection, and then a little more, until she started to request cuddles and even joined Catherine in bed under the blankets. Catherine was also able to take her to visit her parents at weekends, where Milka got full freedom in their garden and honed her hunting skills.

Catherine got a degree in English language, literature and civilization, and her relationship with Milka went from strength to strength until the day she had to make a very tough decision: would she spend a year in the USA teaching French in a primary school, which meant leaving Milka behind with her godmother in Germany, or would she stay in France? It was a decision that would shape her professional life as a French teacher for English-speaking children. She chose to go, and flew Milka to Mainz, on the seat next to her, so she could leave her with her godmother, whose own cat had recently passed over and who was more than happy to have her.

Still, she found it a heartbreaking decision and was worried Milka would forget all about her. But when she returned 11 months later Milka was deliriously happy and couldn't get enough of her love and cuddles. They returned to Toulouse and were able to pick up from where they'd left off.

It was a year later that life changed again. Catherine went to visit a friend in London and fell in love with the man who would later become her husband. They decided to move in together straightaway, but there would be nine months of paperwork, vaccinations, a pet passport and yet more vaccinations before Milka could join them. During this time Catherine decided she wouldn't go back to France to visit Milka, as it would have been too heartbreaking for both of them to be separated again after a visit. She wanted her next visit to be when she would bring her over to the UK to live with her for the rest of her life.

While they were apart, Catherine's mother looked after Milka, but Milka became very depressed because she failed to get on with the resident cats and started to scratch herself to the point where patches of fur were falling out. The day Catherine went to collect her, she was extra-clingy and ultra-affectionate.

At the time Catherine's boyfriend, Trevor, was not a cat-lover, but Catherine had been explicit that she and Milka came as a package and he had agreed. For the first few weeks, though, he refused to allow Milka to even sleep in the bedroom, and Catherine found this hard. However, as she shared, 'Trevor and Milka spent two months observing each other and over this time Milka completely seduced Trevor.'

One night Trevor called to her to come and join him and Catherine on the bed and after that there was no going back. Their house became *her* house and Trevor became *her* daddy. He used to say, 'I still don't like cats, but Milka is a person.'

Trevor and Milka developed a very close bond and he would often have long conversations with her in the kitchen. Milka even learned to play miniature pool: she'd put the ball in the hole then wait for her turn again. She also watched TV, but only animal programmes. She lost interest as soon as humans came back on screen and she was quite indignant if Catherine or Trevor dared change channel. For the remaining six and a half years of her life she lived in a quiet, happy environment where she was very much loved and spoiled.

Catherine regularly visited her family in France and was aware Milka was getting grumpier and grumpier about it. She began to wee or poo on the floor, and even in Catherine's shoes, which she felt was a defiant stand against her absences.

Milka had been gently described as a 'very plump cat' and the vet had instructed that she should eat diet food. But when Catherine returned after spending three weeks in France over Christmas 2009, she noticed Milka had lost some weight. She didn't panic straightaway, but two weeks later when she stroked her she was able to clearly feel her spine beneath her fingers.

After a number of tests, the vet diagnosed acute diabetes and kidney failure. Milka spent a week in the clinic, as the staff did all they could to save her, including injecting her with insulin. Catherine and Trevor went to visit her every day and stayed with her for an hour each time, cuddling her and telling her how much they loved her. It was heartbreaking for them when they had to leave her there and go back to their empty home.

Milka spent another week at home, where insulin injections continued, but nothing was helping her. She was put to sleep two weeks after diagnosis and died in Catherine's arms on the last day of January. Catherine and Trevor were left completely devastated.

When I first saw Milka it was in a headshot photo that Catherine had e-mailed. She had also given me her questions, Milka's age, breed, how long they'd been together and the date of her passing. Everything else would come from Milka directly.

Milka had a serious look in her straw-green eyes and I was hit by a heavy, depressed feeling in my solar plexus, which often indicates to me ill-health, and in some cases emotional imbalance. There was jet black around her eyes and ears then snow-white fur beginning at her neck, creeping up and over her chin and muzzle and meeting between her eyes. What was so distinctive about her facial markings was the black dot placed below the tip of her baby-pink nose and between her whiskers' pads, or puffy areas as some people call them.

I moved past her physical beauty and concentrated on connecting with her soul essence. I felt a strong, maternal presence and gentle, thoughtful character, but I could also feel she didn't suffer fools gladly. She showed me an image of the rest of her body and drew my attention to her white front paws and a white belly. Then I saw her washing herself, an activity in which I felt she took great pride, and lying on Catherine's bed, where it appeared she loved to sleep. I continued to ask her about herself so that I had some impressions I could send to Catherine. She pictured a chenille-type soft material, green or blue dishes and a tree she liked to climb that was positioned in a back garden.

I sent Catherine a collection of impressions and waited for a response.

She replied very quickly, verifying the impressions and explaining, 'There was a burgundy-coloured chenille throw she liked to lie on, and both green and blue dishes. I think the tree was from when she was about three or four, before she came to the UK. There was a cherry tree she loved to climb up when she lived in France.'

Catherine and I arranged a telephone appointment to communicate further with Milka. Her first questions were: 'Will I ever see you and cuddle you again? Will we be reunited one day, either in this life or the next?'

Milka replied, 'Not now, sweet angel. But we will see each other again in the next life.'

'It's reassuring to know I will see her again one day,' Catherine commented. 'Has she been happy with me? Have I loved you enough, Milka, and given you a good life?'

Milka replied, 'Always, dear. Always happy with you. Please – have no regrets. Our life together was perfect.'

'That's such a relief,' Catherine told me, 'as I thought that maybe I had neglected her, especially as I hadn't spotted her health problems early on. I now think she'd hidden them from me for as long as she could. Where is she now? How is it for her out there? Is she loved and looked after?'

Milka replied, 'I'm at peace, my dear. Drifting. Sleeping. Blissful and loved. It's a beautiful place, a beautiful feeling.'

There was a silence on the line as Catherine took a moment to picture Milka in the place she had described. Then she asked her, 'Are you happy?'

Milka gave a simple and complete answer: 'Yes.'

Experiencing a mixture of happiness that Milka was happy and sadness that she was no longer by her side, Catherine questioned, 'Do you miss us and your house?'

'I am beside you more than you know. As you sleep at night, I sit and watch you. I purr you both to sleep.'

'She used to do that,' Catherine happily confirmed. Then she said, 'Are you still with me, even though I can't see you?'

'Yes, often,' Milka replied reassuringly.

Then she gave an image which I described to Catherine: 'She's showing me her ashes. You had her body cremated and the ashes are on a sideboard-type area against a wall. It feels as though it's in the hallway.'

'It is!' she gasped. 'I have created a little memorial for her against the wall in my hallway. I pass it every day. Her ashes are in a box on top of a cloth-covered table where her cat "tree" used to be.'

Milka continued, 'I'm always in your heart. You can connect with me there.'

'When I talk to you, can you hear me?' Catherine wanted to know. 'When I dream about you, is it you communicating with me?'

'I hear you talking,' Milka replied. 'You know I am about.'

Then she added another image. 'This time,' I explained, 'she's showing a picture of herself sitting halfway up the stairs.'

Catherine was stunned. 'I think I'm going mad sometimes,' she admitted, 'because I have seen her there, halfway up the stairs. Definitely. I've seen her waiting for us both to go to bed. When she was alive she used to play with my husband there too.'

Milka added, 'It is easier to reach you in your dreams.'

I told Catherine, 'I get the impression from Milka that you often dream of her outside and enjoying nature.'

'I do dream of her quite often,' Catherine replied. 'There was one dream that was so real. I was talking to her and it was just like talking to her in real life, but it only happened once.'

She paused.

'Is there anything she would like to say to me?'

'Don't worry so much,' Milka said. 'You have a tendency to over-exaggerate emotions. Your emotions are truthful – don't ignore them. But don't make them bigger than they are. You will always remember me.'

I added, 'Milka is giving me the feeling that this is one of your concerns – that you won't remember her.'

'How does she know that?' Catherine asked, surprised. 'Yes, it's true, I have been worried about it. And I do get quite dramatic sometimes.'

Then we reached a concern that many people have: 'Would you be upset or feel betrayed if I ever got a new kitten? Would you allow me to love another kitty?'

'Yes – leap in with all your heart,' Milka affirmed.

'I'm not ready yet to get a new kitty,' Catherine said, 'but her reply is really sweet and I like the prospect of welcoming another cat in my life in the future. Is there anything I can do now to make Milka happy or happier?'

'Just care for yourself – mind, body and soul,' Milka told her. 'As I was always trying to teach you.'

Catherine disclosed, 'This is particularly relevant, as I was diagnosed with multiple sclerosis in 2008, but have suffered MS symptoms since 2000, and I do believe that Milka really helped me through that, both before and after the diagnosis.'

I acknowledged Catherine's honest sharing, then relayed the rest of Milka's answer: 'Live a happy life. Make it happy. Don't always rely on others to make it happy for you. Be proud. Be proud of who you are.'

Through communication, the animals we love are able to reassure us that they do live on beyond death and that their love never ends. The evidence shows that they continue to care about us.

Later Catherine reflected:

'I had always thought that Milka was my baby, but in fact she saw me through many hard times in my life. She was with me during many moves, my studies, lots of jobs and different and sometimes difficult relationships, and was always an incredible support. She has helped me to become an adult and shaped me into the person I am today. She has taught me to be responsible and caring. I was so attached to her and I used to joke I would love to have her surgically attached to me so that she would never leave me. All in all, Milka was the first true love of my life, in the sense that she was the first living creature that I was responsible for and that I had to care for and look after.

I have felt so happy since our communication and am finally feeling peaceful for the first time since Milka passed away. I have been "smiling inside" feeling the warmth of Milka's love and knowing she is happy and at peace. I now feel ready to move on with my life in the knowledge that she will forever be beside me and in my heart.'

Later still, she added:

'With Milka's enthusiastic consent, in May 2010, four months after her death, we adopted an adorable female

ragdoll kitten that I named "Mousse" (for chocolate mousse). I chose a ragdoll because I wanted a cat that looked completely different from Milka and I had read that ragdolls were very affectionate and sociable.

I didn't think I could ever love Mousse as much as I had loved Milka, since we had such an intense relationship, but I still couldn't imagine life without a cat. I was wrong, though: I could love another cat again, and I love Mousse with all my heart. She is a wonderful kitty, sweet, patient and funny, very different from Milka, and both Trevor (who still says he doesn't like cats but that Mousse is a person too, not a cat!) and I have a very happy life with her.

But Milka still is, and always will be, in my heart, and I carry on loving her now as much as I have always loved her. We used to call her mon petit, which means "little one", but the only little thing about her was her size.'

In the next chapter you will hear about Alfie, a rabbit now in spirit form who changed his guardian's life and had a finely tuned sense of prediction.

Chapter 17

Alfie: Best Boy, Best Bunny, Best Friend

'You pay too much attention to what others think. Trust your own feelings more and act on these. This is what will bring you happiness.'
ALFIE

The first animal I ever consciously communicated with was a rabbit. That was back in 2004. Here I was again, years and countless rabbit chats later, with a request from Deborah to communicate with her rabbit, Alfie.

It was the beginning of 2010 when Deborah contacted me from her home in the middle of England. She was managing corporate-level customer service at the time. She wrote:

'I would love you to contact Alfie. He was four years and nearly seven months when he passed over. We'd been together for four years and six weeks.

Please can you let my darling baby boy know I love him just as much as I always have and that I miss him more than words can say? I think of him throughout each day and hope he is happy and safe.

Please let my baby know that no bunny will ever take his place. If I had one wish I would wish for him to be with me again. Words cannot express how much I miss him and love him. And everything I did for him was with love and his best interests were always foremost in my heart. I hope I did the right thing for my baby at the end.

Please also let him know he has been a remarkable teacher and I have grown as a person because of knowing him. My love is as deep for him as always and I hope so much that one day we will meet again.'

The first time Deborah laid eyes on Alfie was in October 2004, in a pet shop. She held him on her lap and they looked at each other for a few seconds.

'He must have seen me for the bunny amateur I was. He gave me a swift nip, leaped into the air and hopped away as fast as he could in a courageous attempt at freedom.

It was at this point that I found myself saying, "I'll have him."

I wasn't entirely sure why I'd said this. There was certainly no way I could have predicted the massive impact this bunny would have on my life. But I'd made my decision and Alfie came home with me the following day as my house bunny.'

Deborah had already tried to get in touch with Alfie via an animal communicator, but it hadn't worked out. She said, 'I didn't feel the person had him – it didn't make sense.' Despite this poor experience, she was willing to give animal communication a second chance. I knew to keep her faith in it I would need to provide concrete impressions that she could verify.

I held Alfie's picture and saw a handsome white dwarf lop rabbit with brindle and tan bursts here and there. He had the breed's signature long, floppy, delicate ears and white paws.

My first impression of him was of a very smiley rabbit with a deep soul. Although he was physically small and compact, there was something all-encompassing about him. He had a large aura and I got the sense that he had been here before – it wasn't his first incarnation. I felt he was capable of reaching into my solar plexus and knowing me. He was fun, mischievous, and I felt he had been gentle with Deborah when still in his physical form. I also felt he liked to have a laugh.

I e-mailed some initial impressions over to Deborah:

'I feel he had a lump along with pain down the left side of his face and upper teeth area; he loved you to hold his ears and admire them; he was a house bunny: he preferred to be in the warm rather than outside; he had a huge appetite and could eat and eat the pellets you gave him; he adored cuddles on your lap and would be very selective about who else touched him. He described an indoor "large wire cage" with lots of "comfort bedding" where he liked to hang out.'

'It all makes sense,' she verified. Then added, 'I gave him a large wire dog cage with blankets in it that he could hop in and out of but was a place of his own.'

'When you called him, he'd come to you.'

'Definitely,' she replied.

Along with the other impressions there was one particular detail that satisfied Deborah that I had connected with her rabbit: 'If there was any flaw in his character it was his obsession with chewing the skirting boards as his teeth grew through.'

'So true!' Deborah agreed. 'He had his favourite places where he'd chew. None of my subsequent bunnies did this – it was solely an Alfie habit.'

Feeling happy with the connection, we arranged a telephone appointment to go through Alfie's communication.

Deborah began, 'Does he visit me? Are there signs I should look for?'

Alfie replied instantly, 'Yes. Feel me on your chest.'

'I've imagined him on my chest!' Deborah exclaimed. 'When he passed initially I thought about him all the time and missed him immensely. I used to lie on the sofa and remember him on my chest and picture him being there with me stroking him. I've longed for him to be with me again, so this gives me a lot of comfort. But where is he?'

'In heaven, of course,' he communicated cheekily. 'Where you want me to be! But I'm here, close by your side too. And everywhere, everywhere you want me to be.'

'Is Alfie happy where he is?'

'Yes, very happy,' he replied. 'No more pain in my mouth. I feel lighter and freer. Carefree, just as you'd want me to be.'

Deborah explained, 'He had a lot of problems with his mouth. He had impacted teeth growing at funny angles and the vet had to clip the ones at the back under anaesthetic. His answer reassures me he's OK.'

We continued with the questions.

'What was the passing over like for him?'

'Not as bad as it was for you. I just relaxed then fell asleep. That's how it is, hopefully. No heart attack. I am peaceful now, so don't worry.'

Deborah said, 'I was with him and he was put to sleep at home, but it was horrendous for me. I do have tremendous guilt. It was such a hard decision – the hardest decision I have ever had to make. He was my little boy. It was so hard to get my head around it, but I knew it was the best way.

'Another thing I would like to know is if I move house, will he still visit me? I can't bear to leave where we lived together, but I will have to shortly, and this worries and saddens me, as our home has so many memories and I feel close to him here.'

Guardians often express concern about moving home when one of their animals has died. The main worry is that they are leaving the spirit of their animal behind, whether that is because of the memories, the energetic presence of the animal or the fact that their body is buried there.

Alfie gave Deborah the reassurance she sought: 'Don't worry about this. Our memories are in your heart. Where you go, I go. Take my picture to remind you. We'll always be together in love.'

'His picture is on my bedroom wall,' she said, 'and I will take it when I go. But will we meet again in this lifetime? And, if so, will he be a bunny and how will I know it's him?'

'Not this one, but definitely the next one,' he replied. 'You'll know me – I'll be the tall, dark stranger. We will fall in love and be together.'

'Human?' Deborah queried.

'Yes,' I told her, 'I believe he's explaining he'll be human.'

There was silence on the phone as Deborah took in this surprising message. It's not unusual for people to believe that animals reincarnate as animals and people as people. But in my view, everything is possible and there are no hard and fast rules in heaven or limitations to reincarnation.

'I would love to know how Alfie felt about his home and me,' Deborah went on. 'Does he have any favourite memories?'

'You are the kindest, sweetest soul and of a sensitive nature. You pay too much attention to what others think. Trust your own feelings more and act on these. This is what will bring you happiness,' Alfie said.

Then he gave an image of perching on the arm or back of a chair and watching TV with Deborah. I asked him what they would watch together and heard the theme tune of *Hollyoaks*. It's not a programme I watch personally (my allegiance is with *Neighbours*), but I catch the trailers occasionally, so I recognized the tune.

Deborah was silent on the other end of the line. Then, astounded, she admitted, '*Hollyoaks* was – and still is – my guilty pleasure. I was in my late thirties when I watched it with Alfie and I didn't tell anyone apart from my husband. Alfie would sit on the back of the chair or lie on the rug and we used to laugh at him with his little back legs stretched out. He would lie with our second rabbit, Poppy, who arrived in 2006, two years after Alfie. They used to look like they were watching TV together.'

At the end of his communication Alfie added a short message: 'Be true in your heart, dear angel. Listen to your own inner being, inner voice, and I will speak to you there. Be gentle, kind and true and you will do well. I will be proud still.'

'It feels so like him,' Deborah said. 'Just before I contacted you I had a dream I was with Alfie and he was healthy and well. It was this dream that spurred me on to e-mail you because I felt as though I was with Alfie for the first time since he'd passed. I felt it was a sign from him that he was around still and OK. I'd had dreams of him before, but when I'd get up close it wouldn't be him, it would be another bunny. That was the only dream that was him totally and utterly, and we recognized each other. He was playing what I can only describe as peek-a-boo around a house and I was following him and when I reached him, I said, "Alfie, is it really you?" His markings were exactly right and the little blonde streaks of fur seemed to glow. He looked so healthy and perfect.'

After the communication Deborah wrote:

'I couldn't stop crying, because not only did it feel like him but you were giving me information that wouldn't have fitted another bunny, so it had to be him. I was overwhelmed with emotion: comfort, sadness, reassurance, longing.

Your communication really helped me to move forward with life again. I felt there must be life beyond for you to come out with details of his wire cage and Hollyoaks, and I was bowled over when you mentioned the lump along the left side of his face. The vets thought it was an abscess initially, but it turned out to be cancer. The fact that you got the correct side and place was incredible.

His personality was so huge that he opened my eyes to just how wonderful, fun and intelligent bunnies really are. He would come when called. He'd ask to go outside or for food. He was cheeky and mischievous and seemed to have a knack for getting into places he shouldn't. He totally owned the house and would hop around, jumping on furniture and racing down the sofa or along windowsills at high speed. He would race to welcome me home, circling my feet in a sign of deep affection. If I'm totally honest, before Alfie, I had no idea that rabbits had so much about them and such depth of character. Alfie changed that. My family had always been dog people and initially I wondered whether Alfie would be enough for me, but he was more than enough – he was the heart of our home. He brought happiness into my life on a daily basis by just being himself and making me laugh, by following me around like a little dog, by licking my foot if I happened to stand by him, by sitting on his back legs like a meerkat. When I talked to him he was so happy he would lick the fur on his chin. He would race up and down the stairs and suddenly make you jump by appearing in the doorway. He'd stop and look at you, then hop over for fuss. He would lie on the bed with me with his little back legs sticking out. We would also lie on the floor together with our legs sticking out and our foreheads and noses touching and I would tell him he was my best boy, my best bunny and my best friend, and he would lick my face or hand to show his love for me.

Alfie showed me how to live completely in the moment and I told everyone about him. He was a rock who was constant through some difficult years in my life: a lonely relationship, the break-up and meeting my wonderful partner, Lee. Alfie was there when I found out I was pregnant and when I nearly died through it being ectopic. Alfie was there when I discovered I would not be able to conceive children naturally and he kept my spirits up during the gruelling IVF. It was about six weeks into the IVF that he began to paw at me frantically and nip me, something he never did. It felt as though he was trying to tell us something and then Lee and I realized he had only ever done this once before – when I had last been pregnant. We felt it could only mean one thing and hoped and prayed he was right. Days later a hospital visit confirmed what Alfie already knew – I was expecting. We were over the moon. Not just once but twice my bunny had known and communicated to me that I was pregnant.

Alfie got me thinking about all the other bunnies out in the world who weren't as fortunate as him, and that prompted Lee and me to adopt Poppy, a beautiful silver-grey and white dwarf lop. Alfie and Poppy were very happy together, but he and I kept our special bond and would spend hours together cuddling.

It is said that with every life there is a death. Our gorgeous son was born in July 2008 and after the difficult time of getting pregnant everything had now fallen into place for me. Yet just two months later Alfie was diagnosed with the most aggressive form of bone cancer on his nose and was given at best a few weeks to live. Initially the vet had diagnosed the lump as an abscess, but this new diagnosis changed everything.

I was beyond heartbroken. I couldn't stop crying and Alfie literally licked away the tears that fell down my face. He was never grumpy and he never showed just how much pain he was in as the growth on his face grew larger each day. He showed me what it was to be courageous and I loved him all the more for his amazing strength of character. He was such an inspiration.

As the days flew by I wanted to capture moments and freeze them in time. I remember sitting with the bunnies, my son and Lee one autumn evening and saying, "This is happiness – being with your family."

Inevitably, Alfie went downhill and I had to make the most difficult decision of my life: to help him pass over to the other side.

The night before, it was as though he knew and was saying goodbye. We must have sat cuddling for two hours, tears pouring down my face and Alfie licking them away and supporting me with his love.

Alfie passed over at home on 6 December 2008 with all of us who loved him at his side. Even in his passing over he led me to Pea and the concept of animal communication. I kept coming across animal communication in books and my husband heard of it several times on the radio and told me about it... it felt as though I was getting little signs. This consultation has not only opened up a wonderful new world for me but also given me the reassurance that Alfie is OK, that there is an afterlife and that one day we will be together again.

I always had a strange knowing, just a gut feeling, that Alfie had been sent to look after me at a time in my life when I needed him, but that when my life was on the right track his time with me would be up and he would have to leave.

I miss him more than words can say. This remarkable bunny taught me so much about rabbits and that they deserve a better life than many get. He taught me that rabbits have just as much personality as other animals. Due to his presence in my life I am less selfish than I was and I have deeper empathy with and compassion for all animals.

I have learned that a strong bond of love and companionship doesn't have to be human – it can come in the form of fur and four legs. My love for Alfie, and his for me, has given me a life-long passion for bunnies, so much so that I have started scribbling my learnings down. My love for both Alfie and Poppy has led to looking after more bunnies, supporting rescues and sanctuaries, meeting some wonderful like-minded people and spreading the word about the wonder of bunnies.'

Synchronicities

Timing is everything. Just before I sat down to write Alfie's chapter I contacted Deborah to check she was still happy for her story to be included in this book. She replied:

'It is funny that I read your e-mail late last night. I have been thinking of Alfie a lot over the last few days. I even saved a little lost bunny on my front drive two weeks ago and guess what his name was? Alfie! I really like to think it was a sign from my boy that he is around me still...

Through Alfie I have learned not to take life for granted and to treasure just being with those I love, four-legged or otherwise, and to truly live in the moment. Since I became more aware I have stopped eating meat and can't believe I ever did now. This cheeky and high-spirited bunny was the most wonderful, loving companion that I could ever have wished for and we shared a bond unlike any other I had experienced before. So would I say I am a better person from having Alfie in my life? Most definitely.'

Animal Sentience

Animals have a much greater perception of physical changes in our body than we do. Alfie knew Deborah was pregnant – twice. Evidence has shown dogs can sniff out illnesses like cancer, epilepsy and diabetes, and they can give advanced warning of blood sugar drops, heart attacks and seizures. In fact, it's been reported that dogs are accurate 97 per cent of the time when million-dollar machines only have a 90 per cent accuracy rate. It's not only dogs, though – cats can detect illness too. At a nursing home in Rhode Island a cat called Oscar knew when someone was about to die and would sit with them offering comfort until they had passed over. He correctly predicted the death of 25 residents.

Given they have so much awareness of what is happening with humans, undoubtedly animals have a great deal of awareness of what is happening with themselves. I'm talking about their perception of their own physicality. Previous animals in this book have explained that they know they are ill and have been able to describe their illness. Some have also been aware they will recover and it's not their time to transition. On the other hand, just this week I came across an owl with a broken wing who knew he was too ill to survive and wanted a quick death so he could fly again on the other side. Humans were desperately trying to save him, but he knew all attempts would fail. They did fail and his suffering was ended with assisted transition the following day.

These experiences need to get us thinking about animals differently. We need to broaden our scope of what animals are capable of understanding. In essence, we need to stop being the 'dumb animal' on this planet and open our eyes to the true intelligence of our co-inhabitants – our animal brothers and sisters.

In the next chapter we head to Egypt to hear the remarkable story of an extraordinary cat called Zanzoun, her special relationship with her guardian and how she was able to soothe her guardian's heart with evidence of her soul's survival.

Chapter 18
Egyptian Zanzoun

'I left my body very early. I hovered over it and watched. I re-entered and waited for the light.'
ZANZOUN

Melissa first made contact by e-mail in February 2009 from her home in Cairo. Her first language was Egyptian Arabic, but her English was beautifully fluent too.

> *'Is it possible for you to alleviate my suffering by giving me news from my beloved cat Zanzoun? She died from a snakebite, during my absence, in agony, which lasted probably for two to three hours. She was a beautiful Egyptian Mau and had only been with us for two years. In that short time she had become mother to two kittens and grandmother to two more. I am so sad that at the time she needed me most I was away.'*

Soon I was sitting with the picture of a jet-black cat in my hand, looking into her vivid pale green eyes and black iris slits. She still looked like a kitten, due to her slender size, but there was something slightly different about her: she didn't have the feel of the many British or American cats I connect with. Zanzoun was slightly distant, even otherworldly.

I took up my pen, connected with her, then began noting initial impressions for Melissa:

'Zanzoun comes across as very athletic, agile and fast.

She was a wonderful mother and very attentive to her kittens – washing them, feeding them and encouraging them to be independent.

She was also a great hunter and able to catch lizards.

There are two homes: one is a block of flats in a city and the other is rural and open.

The flat is very smart, a very large one-floor flat, white or off-white, and has large square tiles on the floor. There is a view over the city from a balcony with a metal rail.

Zanzoun was very affectionate. She adored and respected you. She loved to rub her cheeks against you. She said she claimed you as her own.

She liked to watch what you were doing. She completely trusted you.

She was too adventurous for her own good – it used to get her into trouble.

She liked to sleep on your bed when you were away, because of your scent.

She was also fun and had a mischievous side.

I was amazed when Melissa replied the same day, despite the communication issues of rural Egypt. Although not every detail was correct, the majority were, and Melissa felt I had been able to connect with her Zanzoun.

I'm always interested to hear about an animal's past and how they came to be with their guardian, but I wasn't prepared for the story Melissa revealed in the comfort of a private members' club in central London more than four years after I'd sent her Zanzoun's communication.

'I asked God for the black cat – the one type of cat I'd never had,' she told me. 'I used to be scared of black cats because I was told that people used them for black magic. They're not popular now, but they were in antiquity. All the ancient black cats were revered. And a completely black cat is very Egyptian.'

She told me that Zanzoun's mother had literally dropped her at her door. She had carried Zanzoun and her sibling up a metal spiral staircase all the way to the seventh floor of the Cairo block of flats and could have left them at someone else's door quite easily, but had chosen Melissa's.

Thoughtfully, Melissa placed a cardboard box there to make sure the kittens didn't fall down the stairs.

'I was supposed to leave for England, so I said to our housekeeper, "Please look after them." She wanted the other kitten and I was very happy about that because I thought all the more reason for her to look after the kittens when I wasn't there. But of course she didn't sleep there at night and I couldn't take them into the house – they were too small, the mother was completely wild and I couldn't put my own cats in danger. I left hoping and praying that God would protect them.

At the end of the week I had the terrible feeling that something had happened to my Bengal cat, Tutsi.'

Melissa called her housekeeper to enquire whether anything had happened to him.

The housekeeper said, 'No, he's fine, he's here, everything is well.'

'What about my Siamese cat, Lady?'

'No, she's fine too.'

'What about the little kittens outside and their mother?'

'Well, I think the mother has taken them away and the box has gone.'

When Melissa returned to Egypt three days later, there was nothing there: no box, no kittens and no mother.

'I was exhausted when I got back from London and I was so tired the next morning I decided to have a nap. That's when I had the weirdest dream. I dreamed that the mother had taken her babies and they were drowning. I saw one of the little kittens in black sand and I picked it up. Then all I could see was a blue heart-shaped balloon or cushion-like object floating on water. I felt sad and there was very strange music playing, which I can't put into words. I woke up really startled and thought, I have to go down.'

Downstairs, Melissa asked the doorkeeper, 'Do you know anything about the kittens?' Hearing a noise, she added, 'I can hear a cat meowing!'

He replied, 'Oh yes, that cat has been meowing there for three days.'

Melissa exclaimed, 'Really! Why?' but she was already moving down the stairs to the spot where people stacked up their rubbish to be taken away. The rubbish had been taken away, but a single piece of wood had been left leaning against the wall. Zanzoun was underneath it. Her back half was just lying limp: from the waist down she was paralyzed.

'I picked her up. I was so upset. I held her close to my heart and said, "Don't worry, I will look after you."

Eventually the housekeeper found the other kitten alive and healthy. I don't know what happened to the mother.'

When the vet examined Zanzoun he said, 'Look, I don't want you to get your hopes up because I think the kitten will probably die within two weeks. I suggest you leave her with me, because it's not going to be a nice experience for you.'

Melissa told him, 'God brought that kitten to me and she's my responsibility.'

She took Zanzoun home and looked after her. Zanzoun was given pills to help the nerves to reconnect. And she didn't die – she thrived.

'I was doing healing on her and had no idea if it was working or not. I was putting my hands on her and saying, "God, please channel the energy." In the end, though, she was using her back legs, which was a complete miracle. She could stand up on them and the only thing she couldn't do was move in a complete line – she was more like a sidewinder.'

Zanzoun was about nine months and fully vaccinated when Melissa took her to her country home in Siwa. Her Siamese, Lady, just ignored her, but the other cats took to her because she was still young.

When she was about a year old, an admirer came calling, a rural cat.

'I had never seen anything like it,' Melissa shared. 'I mean, the courtship that went on between those two was just incredible.'

The rural cat was about the same age as Zanzoun and his right front leg had been broken and badly reset so it was permanently turned in. Zanzoun didn't notice – she thought he was wonderful – and he certainly didn't act as though he was handicapped.

'He used to jump about 20 feet from the top of the house to the ground. I have never seen another cat do this. He was really a Superman cat,' Melissa stated. 'He always landed on his four paws.'

One meaning of the name 'Zanzoun' is 'Ethereal beauty' and the rural Romeo certainly agreed with that. Behind the wooden door he would talk to Zanzoun in screechy cat language and she would answer him from her position on the other side.

Melissa said to her housekeeper, 'We'll have to be very careful, because I don't know if Zanzoun can have kittens. It might harm her to do that.'

She contacted the vet for advice. He informed her, 'Yes, I think she can have kittens.'

Melissa wondered whether having kittens would straighten Zanzoun's spine and stretch the nerves back into place.

The vet replied, 'Well, you should do what you feel and see what happens. It should be OK. She's survived so much, it should be all right.'

Melissa told me:

'I don't think I could have stopped it anyway. That cat managed to find Zanzoun wherever she was. He would climb anything to reach her. He even got up on the roof. I had to take her back to Cairo after a while because it was getting very awkward with him around all the time, but obviously they had got married.

I wanted to be there for her when she fell pregnant, but I wasn't there. I wanted to be there when she had her kittens, but I wasn't there then either, because of commitments to my animals on the farm. I'd told the staff to let me know when it happened and I'd told the housekeeper, "Whatever you do, don't pick the kittens up with your hands because you will put your smell on them and then she might reject them. You must put a glove on if you have to handle a

kitten." I had prepared everything before I left for Siwa,
including a big birthing basket. I'd got all the leaflets about
cats having their young and I knew all about it.'

It appeared that Zanzoun gave birth to the first kitten on
Melissa's bedroom floor as she was making her way to the basket.
The second kitten was born in the basket. The first one didn't
move and Melissa's husband thought she was dead, so he told the
housekeeper to get rid of her.

The housekeeper said, 'What! The lady would never say such
a thing. You can't possibly do that.'

Instead she picked the lifeless body up with a glove and gave
it to Zanzoun, and the kitten survived. For this act of kindness
Melissa called this black kitten Safa, after the housekeeper. The
second one, who was a Mau, was, though also a female, named
after the housekeeper's brother, Rafa.

Giving birth didn't affect Zanzoun's disability one way or the
other – it was just the same afterwards. But she was a fabulous
mother and kept the kittens with her all the time.

When they were old enough to walk and had completed their
injections, including for rabies, Melissa asked her husband to
bring them and their mother to her in the country, as they were
needed to keep spiders out of the house.

'One year we had 36 spiders in our country house and
they were the size of tarantulas. One day I was thinking
about killing one because I was scared for the kittens. I
was looking at him as I had that thought and I felt he read
my mind because at that moment he cowered and I heard,
"Please don't kill me, please don't kill me." It was horrible.
So I didn't kill him, I put him in a glass, released him in the
garden and told him, "Don't come back, you're in danger.
Don't come here."

*I think that everything that lives has a soul and that
animals don't need you to talk to them – they read your
thoughts. Insects do, even ants. It's incredible.'*

When her husband pulled up in Siwa, Melissa felt something
wasn't right.

'I don't feel that Zanzoun is with you,' she said.

'She's under the seat in the car,' he said. 'The housekeeper saw
her there.'

'I don't feel she's there,' Melissa stressed.

The housekeeper said, 'Well, she must have run out when we
opened the door.'

'Zanzoun, Zanzoun, Zanzoun,' Melissa called, worried that it
was getting dark. 'I can't feel her.'

Then it suddenly dawned on her. She turned to her husband.

'When did you open the door?'

'When we filled up with petrol.'

'Which petrol station were you at?'

'There were two. The first was just outside Cairo and the
second was at the halfway point.'

Melissa knew immediately: 'The halfway point – that's where
she is!'

*'My husband was very tired and I couldn't ask him to drive
again. Yet it was hopeless trying to sleep and I lay wide
awake worrying. I thought, The longer she's out there, the
less chance I have of finding her.*

*At 2 a.m. I got up and woke our housekeeper, because
I was mad with her. She was the one who had told my
husband, "Yes, I can see her. She's under the back seat."
I didn't care if she was tired too, she was going to have
to come with me. It was very foggy as we climbed into
the car.'*

The housekeeper said, 'We'll never find her.'

Melissa retorted, 'Don't say things like that. Wait until we're there.'

> *'To make matters worse, during our drive there was a terrible sandstorm. I thought, Oh my goodness, what is happening? Everything is trying to stop me from going to Zanzoun. I don't care. I'm going. I just knew I had to be there as soon as I could.*
>
> *We arrived at the petrol station after four hours' solid driving and then spent two hours looking for Zanzoun. I wasn't going to leave until we found her.*
>
> *What I wasn't aware of was that the owner of the petrol station had told his guys, "Just say anything to this woman – she's completely mad, she's come here to search for a cat."*
>
> *They told me, "Actually, there was a lady who came and she thought it was a cute little thing and she took it."'*

Melissa believed them. She thought it was a sign from God that Zanzoun had found a better place than she could offer her. With a very heavy heart she prepared to leave, but before she went she told the garage people, 'If you find her, call me and I will give you a reward.'

It was about noon and they had been driving home for about two hours when Melissa's mobile rang and she heard a male voice say, 'We've found your cat.'

'Where is she?'

'It has crossed the road and it is near where the tank is.'

There was a military tank nearby that had been abandoned after the Second World War on a rectangle of land that divided the sides of a dual carriageway.

Two hours later, when Melissa arrived back at the garage, the men said, 'Look, it's over there by the tank. We'll fetch it.'

Zanzoun was sitting in the shadow of the tank until the man started towards her, then she ran further away.

Melissa replied, 'No, don't go. I'll get her. Don't go.'

Still one of the men kept walking towards Zanzoun, because he wanted the reward.

Terrified she would try to cross to the other side of the carriageway and get run over, Melissa shouted, 'No way! You're going to kill my cat. If you do, you'll get no reward. So you come back here.'

With the threat of no reward, the man stopped dead in his tracks.

Melissa crossed to Zanzoun, who sat quietly waiting to be picked up, just as she had when she was a kitten, scooped her straight up to her heart and returned to her car.

'I took her back home, which took another four hours. I was wearing a white blouse and when I arrived home I realized there was red on it. I believe the men had tried to catch her and they had grabbed at her so hard she had been bleeding. When I had held her over my heart, her blood had marked my blouse.'

Despite all this, Zanzoun recovered well from her ordeal. She was so happy to be back home.

Everybody else thought Melissa was mad. People kept saying, 'I would never go all that way for a cat!'

She simply replied, 'She's *my* cat.'

It wasn't long before Zanzoun and her kittens grew up. Her firstborn, Safa, was large and very sensible, and her second daughter, Rafa, was very rough. In less than two years Melissa had actually three generations of cats in the house:

'*Safa had two kittens, a female we named Pandora and a male we named Zuka. The male disappeared the day we decided we were going to have him neutered. I felt him tell me, "No, you're not doing that to me. I choose my freedom."*

I told him, "You'll be so much happier if you have the operation. You'll have an easy life, less fighting – just look at the cats who are torn to bits." But it seemed I couldn't convince him. The country vet works with cows, goats and horses and doesn't think cats are worth bothering about. Our nearest vet who knows about cats and dogs is eight hours away in Cairo. He came to neuter some of my other animals, but Zuka didn't reappear and present himself.

When the vet had left, I still didn't know where Zuka was but I said to him, "The vet's gone, you've missed it."

I heard him repeat, "I choose my freedom."

I never saw him again.'

A year later Melissa and her husband made another trip to England.

'When I left, I told the housekeeper *never* to leave Zanzoun in the garden,' she said. 'She always had to come in.'

Sadly, it didn't work out that way.

Melissa explained, 'The local people were terrified to go into the garden to get her when it was dark. They were scared of ghosts, devils and *jinns*.'

Jinns, also called genies, like the one that comes out of the lamp in the story of Ali Baba, can be mischievous spirits but can also be neutral towards humans or even benevolent. They have free will, just as humans do.

Nevertheless, Melissa recalled, 'The guards at our house in Cairo would pee in the front doorway rather than walk 40 feet away because of their fear of the *jinns*. They were terrified they would come into their body and possess them.'

So, when Zanzoun was in the garden and darkness fell, the housekeeper was too scared to go out and look for her.

On her return from England Melissa rang her when she was in the car travelling back to her Cairo home.

'So, how are my cats?'

'Oh, the cats are fine.'

'How is Zanzoun?'

'Oh, she is right in front of me. Zanzoun is right in front of me.'

> *'But she wasn't. The housekeeper had left her out all night. She'd thought she would get away with it because Zanzoun would be waiting by the door the next morning. But the garden is full of vipers and a cat who hears the movement of a snake will be interested. And Zanzoun was handicapped, so not in total control of her movements.'*

The next day Zanzoun was discovered in the garden.

'That morning I saw it in my coffee cup,' said Melissa. 'Just as people read tea leaves, I read coffee grounds, and I saw a black cat there. I wasn't happy about that.'

She rang her Siwa home.

'How is Zanzoun?'

Sobbing, the housekeeper replied. 'She is dead. The gardener found her.'

> *'I went to the country the next day, which was as quickly as I could get there. I was on fire, absolutely on fire. I was in so much pain I didn't know what to do – it was as if it was oozing out of me, a burning feeling. It was a huge reaction, completely over the top, but I am over the top in my love for animals.'*

Melissa's niece had consulted me about her own missing cat and she passed her my contact details. After sending over my first impressions of Zanzoun for her to verify, I e-mailed the full communication:

> *'In the communication there is a quiet superiority and wisdom, as if Zanzoun knows things. I feel you were together for a reason. To me, Zanzoun feels like a magical animal; she has special powers. I also feel her destiny was to have a short life. She knew this and that was why she lived life to the full.*
>
> *Zanzoun wants you not to worry. She pictures herself hunting in long grass, almost panther-like. She now has great strength and speed and she is with a white cat who has longer fur.'*

Melissa replied:

> *'Everything you said was mind-boggling. Zanzoun described my home in Cairo and my garden in the countryside. She described her human father coming in from work wearing a suit and the big tiles on the floor. She told you I had a grown-up daughter and son who both lived away from home, which is true. How did she know that? Or should I say how did you know that? How did you get that from the cat? I thought the first thing you would say when you communicated with Zanzoun was "That cat was handicapped", but as I read your communication I realized that Zanzoun never thought of herself as handicapped. That was a revelation to me. She never saw herself as handicapped at all.*
>
> *I had previously said to myself, "If Zanzoun is truly a magic cat," as I felt she was, "then she will have her*

opposite, yin and yang, to receive her at the other end."
This was a thought that came to me. I thought it was
completely crazy, but now I know she is with a white cat, it
does make sense.'

The vet decided to have Zanzoun's body autopsied. Melissa
hadn't requested it and felt he was just keen to make money. She
told me what happened when she returned to her country house:

'They had already buried her by the time I arrived. I felt
that it was maybe better that way, because with the poison
she had been totally blown out of proportion.

I visited the spot where the accident had happened and I
noticed there were areas where the sand was different, as
if something had rolled over on it. This upset me no end, as
I felt the poor cat must have been in agony. The vet told me,
"Yes, she would have died in absolute agony because the
poison made her liver and kidneys split."

Then you wrote that Zanzoun wanted to explain how she
had died.'

Zanzoun had given me a message for Melissa:

'I did not have the agony he spoke about. That was not
me, it was my body that stretched and contorted while I
waited outside. I left my body very early. I hovered over it
and watched. I re-entered and waited for the light. It came
quickly and a man walked out to me and gestured for me
to go with him. I went. He had a kind energy.'

Melissa said:

'The things that you said made me cry for ages afterwards.
Every time I told the story I was in tears. I knew she had

been bitten on the head, but you also told me she had been bitten on her left paw. The vet had missed the second snakebite, but both the gardener and housekeeper told me she had been bitten on the left paw and they had found her with her left paw in her mouth.'

Zanzoun had more to say to Melissa:

'Tell Melissa I love her and not to worry. Tell her to look after the kids and I will come by to see how they are doing. They will look up to me, into an empty space, then you'll know I am there.'

Melissa acknowledged:

'This is exactly what happened. The kittens and I were on my bed and then suddenly they both looked up at the same spot in the air.

That cat gave me so much and I absolutely adored her.'

This story shows the lengths people will go to for their animals and that the deep bond of unconditional love is not broken by death. Zanzoun teaches us that animals can thrive despite disability, that there is more to dying and death than meets the eye, and that cats are loyal too, as she communicates to soothe the soul of her devoted guardian and replace her agony and guilt with love.

In the final part we explore *living life with love*. This is the message animals repeatedly give their guardians and one they wish to share with the world. The first chapter begins with a golden retriever named Geneviève, but also involves a rook named Borvis and a wild rabbit named Pears.

Part VI

LIVING LIFE
WITH LOVE

*'In order to learn the art of dying, one must
know – completely – the art of living.'*
S. N. GOENKA

Chapter 19
Geneviève, Queen of Hearts

༺৯৹

'Focus on the joy rather than the loss.'
Geneviève

It was in a little place called Ballydehob in West Cork, Ireland, that I first met Jennifer and heard about her golden Labrador, Geneviève. I'd been giving an animal communication workshop there and during lunch we sat outside and talked about our aged dogs. That was in 2010. In May 2011 Jennifer asked me to connect with Geneviève because she felt too emotionally entangled to do so herself.

Before you read about Geneviève's soul journey, allow Jennifer to share how Geneviève came to her, her husband, Peter, and their three children, who were aged five, eight and nine at the time:

'We found a litter on a farm outside Bandon. The nine six-week old pups squealed and snuffled – it was joyous pandemonium. A female pup came and sat next to me, but I took little notice of her, as we had our minds set on a male dog.

I moved to another part of the barn, prompted by the excitement of my children, and the little female pup followed me. As I squatted amidst the puppies, she sat down next to me, seemingly unperturbed by the ruckus.

I moved again, and again she followed to sit next to me. By this point, I couldn't help but take notice of her. She was following purposefully, although she wasn't even looking at me.

I called to the children over the chaos: "I think this one is determined to come home with us!"

The children named her "Geneviève" after a golden dog who rescues mischievous Madeline from drowning in a children's book. Ironically, my mother wanted to call me that name but was told it was too "foreign". It's so close to my own name, though, that when someone called Geneviève, I often thought they were calling me.

We lived in the countryside, where our children were home educated, so the puppy quickly became a significant part of their daily lives. They adored her.

Much time was spent in the car travelling to music lessons, rehearsals and performances, and Geneviève always joined us. On the long drives home in the evening, especially in the winter months, I began to make up stories about her to "shorten the road". In this way the children playfully became aware that Geneviève was more than "just the family dog". In the stories she continually reminded them, "I am not a dog." Nor, she reiterated, did she belong to anyone. Instead, she was a vast, all-knowing being.

My imagination aside, Geneviève clearly had a developed sense of humour, as Labradors often do, which engaged the children fully. They chattered to her constantly, climbing into her basket to play, and she joined them on races across the fields, down to the sea, in the garden or chasing the football – she was a part of the pack.

Not all in the family were overjoyed by Geneviève's arrival, though. Peter, who was frequently travelling overseas with his work, wasn't happy to meet her. I had long spoken of having a dog, but while he was away I'd had a very strong impression to act on it immediately. I couldn't explain why and Peter was understandably perturbed that he had not been part of the process or the selection of the pup. It caused considerable discord when all I could keep returning to was "But the puppy kept following me" and "It was as though she was meant to be with us."

He also disliked the chaos surrounding life with a puppy. He thought home education was enough to cope with and it was ludicrous to add a chewing, yapping puppy. Perhaps in response to this, Geneviève indeed became "the puppy from hell", tearing around the sitting room, whose antique pine floors Peter had lovingly sanded and varnished, her puppy toenails gouging into the wood; playfully snapping at anything in sight, including the children; climbing onto the kitchen table to devour a loaf of freshly baked bread then vomiting it everywhere.

Peter was far from thrilled with her. When she was six months old, he asked me if I would find another home for her because she was "too wild". I reluctantly agreed on one condition: if I could shift her behaviour in the next three months, we would keep her. I engaged help from a friend who is a seasoned dog trainer and became very disciplined with Geneviève's training. She responded quickly. We *changed her diet to raw meat, raw vegetables and bones, and her behaviour calmed. At the end of the three-month trial, nothing further was said.*

We took her everywhere with us. She and I walked daily across several fields and through holes in hedgerows to the sea, and the children scratched illustrations of her adventures on flat stones on the beach.

Over the years, besides being an integral part of the home-schooling pack, she became my closest companion. We had long philosophical discussions on our daily walks, she'd lean her warm golden body into mine if I were upset, she'd make me laugh at her futile attempts to catch flies and she'd rest her head on my hand on the gear stick, making it impossible to shift as I drove.

When she was five, armed with a PET passport we drove to Italy to live on a dilapidated 17th-century biodynamic farm outside Florence. Geneviève befriended everyone there.

By the time she was nine, we had moved to a village in Portugal, where she had her first taste of restricted access: our neighbours had a pair of fierce, bullying Rhodesian ridgebacks who terrorized the pacifistic Geneviève. Fortunately, there was an expansive national forest above the village, so Geneviève and I resumed our long walks there.

When she was about 12, someone knocked at the front door one day. I heard her bark an announcement, but she didn't come rushing to see who it was, as was her habit. I discovered her on the ground, legs splayed, unable to move, gazing at me helplessly. The local vet suggested arthritis, but our homoeopathic vet back in Ireland, Tom Farrington, who took a complete history, saw this as the beginning of kidney trouble. I fed her sardines for the oil, massaged her hips and gave her a series of homoeopathic remedies. Although she improved a little, she began to have difficulty getting into the car and climbing stairs, and she started to flag on our walks, which had to be considerably shortened.

When she reached 13, Peter and I returned home to Ireland. The children were now away at university. Geneviève was visibly happy to be home – something in her slow, deliberate gait and demeanour exuded a sense of comfort and familiarity. I noticed her left hip was giving her more trouble, she was losing weight and often seemed cold. The vet confirmed her kidney trouble and treated her with further homoeopathic remedies. Nevertheless, after a few months at home, it was clear she was rapidly deteriorating.

One winter evening, as she walked slowly from the kitchen to her basket in the conservatory, I saw her stop midway. She looked around, tried to walk backwards, stopped and looked completely disoriented. Her eyes were far away, then began blinking rapidly. I spoke to her, but it was as though she didn't hear me. Our vet confirmed she was having a seizure, which is a symptom of uraemia. I gave her a high potency homoeopathic remedy, brought her to her basket and she slept. The next day, it was as though nothing had happened – she was on fine form.

Peter had warmed to her over the years, but he would still be the first to find fault with her. Her bi-annual shedding irritated him no end; her barking announcements were always "too loud". Her love gradually worked on him, however, and in her last few years their relationship underwent a radical transformation. The more he let go of his resistance to her, the more he could clairvoyantly see her radiance, a warm yellow glow that emanated from her heart. As her health degenerated, he gently and compassionately cared for her.

I also began to experience my heart in a very different way – as if there were a slow-motion tsunami building inside it. When I fed Geneviève, walked her or just sat close talking to her, my physical heart seemed to expand laterally, to encompass a greater area. There was an interchange of warmth and depth passing back and forth between us. I knew that I would do absolutely anything for her – not in a rational, practical sense, but in a vast unconditional sense. I was wide open.

When cataracts formed over her eyes, we put a small solar light in a jar by her basket so when she wandered back to it in the dark, she'd have a little glow to remind her where it was.

Our walks were now confined to the garden. She seemed interested in little more as she limped along, just seeming to endure it and spending much of her day sleeping.

At Christmas, however, when the children returned home, she made Herculean efforts to accompany the family on a long walk through the snow. It was both heartwarming and heartbreaking to watch her take her place with her much-loved pack. When the children left, she sank back into a depressed routine of sleeping and taking a few steps around the garden. She had further seizures; each time the homoeopathy seemed to help, but the recovery time grew longer.

One day I had the strong impression that we needed to drive 45 minutes to see her vet, Tom. This was irrational;

she was old, weary, and no longer enjoyed being in the car, as the narrow, winding roads jostled her too much. Our recent consultations with the vet had been solely over the telephone. To think of driving Geneviève to the surgery, a 90-minute round trip, seemed ludicrous, but I felt compelled.

She seemed to be happier than usual to get into the car. Although she was always agitated in the surgery, panting and pacing, when we arrived she hurried to Tom and nudged him for contact.

He was kind as usual, but quickly moved on to the business of helping Geneviève medically. He trawled through pages on the internet, hunting for a particular remedy. Geneviève continued to nuzzle him, insistent upon getting his attention, but Tom was engrossed. She left his side, walked out to the car through the open door and lay down. I looked at her. She looked back then put her head down as though in resignation. I questioned why I had brought her.

Frustrated at feeling the visit was futile, as Tom himself had suggested there wasn't much left to do for her, I mentioned how much I wished to know what Geneviève was feeling and how to best serve her in her remaining time – I hungered to communicate with her.

After hunching over his computer with acute mental focus, Tom abruptly bolted upright and said brightly, "You should contact an animal communicator. I recently did a workshop with an extraordinary one. Her name is Pea Horsley and she's based in England. She's actually teaching a workshop this spring – come to think of it, in your village."

That spring, Jennifer attended my workshop in Ballydehob. She arrived with photos of Geneviève, yearning to learn how to listen to her. However, she was concerned that she might not be able to distinguish her own emotional projection from Geneviève's unadulterated message:

'With the teachings at the workshop, I discovered I seemed to have some facility for listening to other people's animals, but could I do this as effectively when I went home to Geneviève? I longed to know how she was in herself, beyond the physical discomfort of her body's degradation. I wanted to hear her final wishes and whether she required assistance from our vet.

I practised regularly with wild animals and found their communications short but very clear. However, when I went to Geneviève, I quickly began to doubt myself. Was I blocking my own ability to hear her? When I returned from the workshop I could feel she was overjoyed with what I was doing, but when I went to ask how she was specifically, I couldn't receive a clear response.'

By now, Geneviève could hardly walk. It was a glorious spring, though, and Jennifer was able to carry her outside to lie on the grass:

'In these weeks, I can only describe the feeling as becoming one with her. Where she began, I ended; where she ended, I began. My heart stretched ever wider. Her eyes were dim, but I know she still saw me. There were occasionally tiny flickers of light through her weary, heavy-lidded black eyes and her tail still made tiny twitching movements when I approached her.'

Geneviève deteriorated further: she became unable to control her bladder or bowels and was no longer interested in eating more than a mouthful of meat. She was becoming dehydrated, the skin around her nose and eyes was cracking and she had frequent nosebleeds. Jennifer was helping her to drink, cleaning her and changing bedding constantly.

> *'I was happy just being with Geneviève, but when my neighbour said, "You just have to do the deed, Jennifer, you can't have her suffering like that," I wobbled. Was I selfishly perpetuating her suffering?*
>
> *It was at this critical point, when "reason" began banging at my door, that I contacted Pea for clarity around Geneviève's final wishes.'*

I printed Jennifer's e-mailed photos of Geneviève. One showed the soft face of a golden Labrador, another her lying in her wicker basket, head up, sunbathing, with a rook crouched to her left, facing the same direction, and a third was a close-up of the same rook next to a bowl of water.

Jennifer told me she had tried to ask his name and heard 'Aster.' Then she realized he was communicating, 'Ask her,' referring to Geneviève. When she did this, she clearly heard 'Borvis.' Out of curiosity she web-searched the name and discovered it had a Yiddish meaning: 'barefoot'. There was also a Romanian reference to mineral water and changing water to wine, and an American online gaming reference to 'the Dragons of Borvis', who were notorious for their shapeshifting ability. Jennifer was already aware that in Native American traditions the rook governed magic and was the one to give courage to enter the darkness of the void – all that was not yet in form.

She explained that two weeks earlier, on a cloudless, warm day, a large old rook had flown onto the low stone wall just outside the kitchen. 'He had a well-worn scratched beak, scruffy feathers – he was quite comical, like a wizened old man in tattered black trousers, but full of energy.' He strode up and down the wall then stopped and lowered himself on his 'haunches' to sit quietly.

The next day, he reappeared. He hopped down to the patio and strutted confidently, drinking from Geneviève's water bowl.

Unperturbed by Jennifer's presence, he kept returning day after day, and each day seemed to feel more at home. He began to approach Geneviève, either lying on the grass or outside in her basket, to the point where one day he sat right next to her. Geneviève lifted her head, looked squarely at him and there was 'a feeling of recognition'.

On another warm day, Geneviève was lying on the kitchen floor with the door open. Jennifer left the kitchen for a moment and returned to discover the rook perched on the back of a kitchen chair, looking down at Geneviève and clucking very quietly, almost purring.

'Geneviève looked up at Borvis,' Jennifer said, 'then put her head down as though this was nothing out of the ordinary.'

When I first found the stillness to connect with Geneviève, the overarching impression was one of grace. This was closely followed by gentleness, humility and loving kindness. I could also sense she was generous and had great strength of will. Geneviève came across as a very happy soul who was here for a purpose – to empower – and that included not only family but friends as well. I wrote on my notepad: 'She's a queen.'

I felt Geneviève was very tired physically, emotionally and spiritually and that she needed to recharge 'through death'. I felt she had prayed for the energy to continue life as long as possible and Borvis had arrived as support. But I knew she was just waiting for death.

When I connected with Borvis I felt he had come in service to Geneviève and that they had been together in another lifetime. He was watching over her now and telling her of 'light-work' to be done on the other side.

Geneviève also communicated to me, 'All is well,' and, 'Tell her I feel loved. I always have.'

I sent these impressions across to Jennifer, who verified them and accepted the description I gave of Geneviève. We immediately moved on to her questions.

'Are you in pain?'

'No. You kindly make no fuss,' Geneviève replied.

'Do you wish us to have Tom, our vet, put you down or do you wish to go on your own?'

'Let me go naturally,' she replied. 'This is the journey of life and death. Everything in its own time. No pain. No shame. It will be perfect.' Then she added, 'Tell Tom *no!*'

I didn't know what that meant, but passed on the message for Jennifer to decipher.

'Is there any way we can assist your passage? Do you wish to be left outside on the grass? Do you wish to be left alone to make your transition?'

'Be close if you can. You'll find it peaceful to see my spirit leave. Do not worry what others say. Our hearts are true to each other.'

When I was repeating Geneviève's answers, Jennifer admitted she was under a lot of pressure to give her an assisted transition.

'If you do not wish assistance to cross over, can you give us an idea of your own timing?' she asked. Then she went on to explain, 'We have to go away for three weeks and if you are still here I will need to make arrangements.'

Geneviève's reply was short: 'No, I can't.'

I told Jennifer my feeling was that Geneviève would transition soon and it could be within the next week.

At this point I felt an urge to ask Geneviève my own question: 'Do you know what is happening?'

She replied, 'I am slipping away. It feels like sliding. Nothing will stop it.'

I could feel this sensation was slow, not fast or scary, just inevitable.

Jennifer wanted to ask about further practical matters, 'Do you have a preference as to where you would like to be buried? In the orchard? To the east or west, north or south? Near the house? Near Borvis?'

I asked about Borvis's transition and Jennifer explained:

'One afternoon as I crossed the patio I saw him perched on the wall, not far from where Geneviève was lying on the grass. I opened my heart to him.

"Sit!" he commanded.

I was quite taken aback and sat.

"Close your eyes. Now focus," he told me.

I did and fell into a deeply meditative state. It was as though the garden had become a boundless space. I was filled with the sense that I was connected to everything.

Fifteen minutes passed, though it seemed timeless, and as I opened my eyes I heard, "You'd be wise to move more slowly."

I stared at Borvis. He looked much bigger than a rook, as though a presence had surrounded him and enlarged his appearance.

Unbeknownst to me, Peter had had an almost identical experience with Borvis just a few hours earlier. We marvelled when we compared notes and agreed he was undoubtedly a teacher.

After he'd lived with us for 12 days, sitting next to and seeming to commune with Geneviève, we found him lying on his side by Geneviève's water bowl. It had been unseasonably hot, so we thought he might be suffering from heatstroke, given his seeming great age.

Peter picked him up and we sprinkled him with water, gave him drops to drink and brought him into the shade under a cherry tree. His claws clutched at Peter's fingers for a moment and he stared at him then slowly released his grip. He was dead.

We felt it best to leave his body lying in the shade for a while to allow him to transition undisturbed. We lit a stick of incense, put a small purple flower on his breast and offered him our love. Peter saw his spirit rise from his lifeless body to overlight the entire garden and connect to Geneviève.

A few minutes later, we were astonished to see Geneviève get up and walk – shakily, but with a pointed determination – to the cherry tree. She sat down, head high, like a sphinx, and remained there, radiant, for the next four hours, as though keeping a vigil. Afterwards, she limped back to her basket. She never walked again.'

It was a moving revelation and there was so much to take in. I felt Borvis had come to show Jennifer what death was and also to honour Geneviève's wishes. I could sense they had communicated with each other about their next life together and how Geneviève felt about leaving Jennifer.

I repeated Jennifer's question: 'Do you have a preference as to where you would like to be buried?'

'Large apple tree – horizontal branches, very old, large trunk. The Earth Tree: holding the energy. It receives a lot of sunshine. It's where the bright star is.'

Geneviève showed an image of a star shining brightly and I felt a link to Jerusalem and Jesus. It felt as though the tree was in a southerly direction.

Jennifer said, 'I know that tree. About 10 years ago a very old Bramley apple tree toppled to the ground in the southeast corner of the garden. We assumed it would die but it continued to grow, spreading its branches horizontally and bearing abundant fruit each summer.'

Geneviève offered a final message for each member of the family.

'I can't stop my tears, as the messages are so accurately designed for the individual histories and personalities,' Jennifer observed.

To Jennifer herself, Geneviève said:

'We are one and of the same energy, from the same soul group. We are helping each other evolve, discovering new depths to our spirits. All is well with us. We have learned so much through each other and will continue to do so. It doesn't end, not here. My love continues. You will feel me in your heart. Look up to the bright star and you will see me. All I have wanted to say to you, I have said. I have told you through my eyes... Our love has always been pure, from many lifetimes ago. Know your heart is always strong enough. I feel loved and always have.'

Towards the end of her communication she added that she had a message for Tom. I got the sense she had to activate something in veterinarian Tom, but he needed to take the first step.

Geneviève concluded her communication with another message for Jennifer: 'You have always done the very best for me. Love. God bless.'

Finally, I received an image of the number 16 in Roman numerals: XVI. I shared this with Jennifer, although I had no sense of its meaning.

Later Jennifer explained to me that the previous Wednesday Geneviève and Borvis had appeared 'larger than life' in Tom's morning meditation – Geneviève's face with Borvis behind her – with the urgent message that he come to see her. He told them that in his 30 years of veterinary practice with hundreds of animals and as someone who had had countless dogs and cats as pets himself, he had never had such an experience. It startled him, so he took it seriously and set out to see Geneviève right away. However, he got hopelessly lost on the winding country roads. He rang the house four times, but Peter was on the telephone with a client all evening, so he was unable to get through. Thereafter he was fully engaged with his veterinary practice until the following Sunday.

By then Geneviève was undeniably slipping fast. Her body was lifeless, her functions all failing. She could still move her eyes and her head just a bit, but her lifelong wagging tail had ceased even twitching. Jennifer told me:

'On Sunday morning I noticed she kept making the effort to raise her head to see over the rim of her basket, out of the window and up the road.

Tom arrived at midday. When his car rolled down the road to the house, she looked at me and I saw a bit of light in her eyes.

Tom and Geneviève spent 20 minutes together. He said he felt a stream of warmth pouring from her into his heart and saw it as a long optical tube of light. He told us she might have three or four days left and asked if he could offer her some hydration. I naively agreed, as I imagined him filling a dropper with water, and was then appalled to see him go to the car and return encumbered by medical trappings to intravenously hydrate her.

I looked at Geneviève and though her eyes were faded, I received a very clear impression of 'No.'

As I went to say something, Tom put his hand by her head and Geneviève growled and snapped at him. She had never snapped at anyone, except as the wildly chewing puppy. Tom was shocked she had the strength to do so and quickly accepted that she didn't want to be given anything.

I relayed Geneviève's message from Pea: "Tell Tom no." She wanted to go completely unassisted.

As we sat with her, Geneviève continued to beam light into Tom's heart.

Tom warned us that with uraemia the toxins being released into the brain might cause Geneviève to die shrieking and it might go on for a few days. Could we take it?

I was grateful for his concern, but had taken great comfort in the messages Geneviève had relayed through Pea and assured him, "All is well." He was very happy to hear we had consulted Pea and felt moved by what he perceived as the gift he had been given by Geneviève.

I received the impression from Geneviève that she wanted me to stay nearby, so I moved my work into the conservatory to be next to her. But soon after Tom left, both Peter and I were overcome by an intense and inexplicable drowsiness. We both went into the sitting room and fell asleep. It was bizarre.

About 20 minutes later, I awakened with a start to see a cloud of tiny shimmering light crystals surrounding me. Peter awoke and we both saw a shot of light streak across the sitting room. Then we heard a gagging sound and immediately went to Geneviève. I wanted to tell her I loved her. "Oh, sweetheart" was all I could manage, but I felt remarkably clear and still.

Within 10 minutes, her whole body went into short, sharp spasms. She lifted her head, took a breath in, let it out and everything stopped. Grace. Perfection.

Peter sobbed uncontrollably.

With regard to the Roman numbers XVI, using the 24-hour clock these numbers correspond to 16:00. Geneviève died at 4 p.m. It became clear to us she had been waiting for Tom.

Peter saw her spirit rise and join that of Borvis, whose light had continued to overlight our garden. I placed flowers in her basket, lit a beeswax candle then took myself on the walk that Geneviève and I had taken together for years, through the holes in the hedgerows, across the fields and down to the sea.

I was hollowed out, but there were no tears left in me. I sat on the beach and everything felt flat. I spoke to Geneviève, remembering aloud so many things we had done. As I did, it felt as though I was looking down a tunnel, unemotionally witnessing the events of our lifetime together.

A large seagull began circling over my head, flying lower and lower until he was only three or four arm's lengths above me. Moments later, a rook flew so close by I felt the rush of his wings. He was squawking. Then a tiny sparrow alighted on a rock next to me and stared at me. The message I received was: "All is well. We are here."

That evening, Geneviève's spirit continued to waft around me in the living room. We also noticed that there appeared to be waves of energy rippling across her body. It almost looked as though she was still breathing. We felt no rush to bury her – what seemed important was just to sing our hearts to her. The candle burned all night and was still alight the next morning, strangely only melted halfway down. There was a beautiful but subtle odour in the conservatory where Geneviève lay.

In between torrential downpours, we buried her where she had requested in the southeast corner of the garden by the Earth Tree. Peter was very emotional; he had been on such a steep learning journey with her, one that had ended in a wash of love.

The night of her burial I dreamed of two complete rainbows, one above the other. As I looked at them, they merged into one colossal, resplendent rainbow. I wondered if they represented Geneviève and Borvis's energies merging together.

The last impression I received from her after the burial was: "Focus on the joy rather than the loss."

For weeks after, I continued to feel her presence in the house and garden. There was lightness to it, unlike the heaviness of the degenerating body she had inhabited. About three months later, when she would have been 14, her presence became more internalized – rather than surrounding me, it was a feeling focused inside my heart. I literally felt it as a glowing ember, a radiance.

Peter saw Geneviève's spirit bounding around the garden in youthful form and Tom telephoned to say Geneviève had appeared to him in a meditation as a puppy.

In Pea's communication with Geneviève, I had asked if she would ever join me again, as I dreaded the imminent void of her departure. Geneviève showed Pea an image of *a rabbit and then Pea heard her say, "A bird," and, "You would know me if I walked through your door. You'd know me immediately."*

Our garden was often peppered with wild rabbits, particularly since Geneviève had become infirm and no longer able to chase them. Several days after her transition, I noticed a single rabbit who didn't scatter with the rest when I appeared but seemed uncharacteristically fearless. Each time I saw him, I stopped and tried to open my heart to him. It wasn't difficult, as I felt the ember of Geneviève begin to glow in my chest. I heard his name was "Pears" and he had highlights in his coat the colour of Pears soap.

Like Borvis, he was a teacher and also a taskmaster. He'd stop what he was chewing on, sit back on his haunches, become perfectly still and we would meditate together. The moment my focus strayed, he'd be off like a shot, showing me what focus actually was by disappearing when I lost it.

When I asked him if he was Geneviève, he simply replied, "We are all one."

As our communication developed, my gratitude and joy deepened – I felt as though my heart was beginning to open in a way I had known as a child.

A few months later, I travelled to the New Mexico desert to shoot a film I had spent three years developing. Peter only saw Pears a few times in the orchard after I left.

While away, I went through a challenging time with work. Deadlines were approaching, the remaining funding wasn't materializing, an actor we were counting on was being elusive, our cinematographer was backing out and I was questioning whether the project would come to fruition. I began to doubt myself, my abilities and my vision.

Early each morning before it became too hot, I walked along a deserted railroad track in the open wilds to sit quietly and meditate before the day's frenzy took over. One morning as I walked, a wild white-winged dove flew from a tree several yards ahead of me, landed on my shoulder and began cooing in my ear and tenderly pecking at my shoulder. Dumbfounded, I slowly lowered myself to sit on the ground without disturbing her. When I sat, she hopped to my arm, onto my knee and then to the ground in front of me. Our eyes met, she bowed and cooed and began circling me as though performing a mating ritual. Everything around me disappeared: all I was aware of was love. Tears burned my eyes in wonder and I had the impression of Geneviève. I recalled Pea hearing Geneviève say she would appear as a bird. "You would know me if I walked through your door. You'd know me immediately." My heart flew open.

The dove flew to me for the next six days on my morning walks. The impression I was given on each visit was: "All is well," along with the feeling of love. And all was well: at the risk of sounding trite, the film did fly and was actually driven by love.

It is a sacred privilege to know animals and, further, to learn to listen to them. For this, I have Geneviève to thank – for lifelong teaching, for the golden glow that lives on in my heart – and Pea, who has already learned to listen with her heart and is willing to share what she hears and encourage others to remember and listen.

When darkness falls, the small solar light jar, which still lives in the conservatory, comes alight. It is a perpetual reminder that Geneviève's light shines on.'

Chapter 20
The Black Dog

27 January 2012

It's exactly six months since Morgan ascended. There are still tears because I miss his physical presence in my life, but I can now look back on the happy memories and smile, remembering how he'd run off, be very stubborn and pull on the lead to reach a tiny crumb virtually invisible to the human eye. I remember him being good at sharing his bed with his canine pal Roxy: she'd lie in his and he'd lie in hers.

Morgan only had two doggie friends and they were both girls: Saffie, a pretty golden retriever, and Roxy, a stunning red heeler. It was a sad moment and the end of an era on 25 January when Roxy had a seizure and transitioned to the Light. Saffie, who had been battling with cancer, had been gently assisted out of her bleeding, tired body the previous November. Within six months of Morgan's transition both his girlfriends had joined him.

The Black Dog Appears

All the time I was grieving the physical loss of Morgan there were signs of his successor. As sure as day follows night and the birds sing up in the trees, the black dog found me.

For 11 months I discouraged Jo from looking for a dog because emotionally I just wasn't ready. Then, when we were travelling across Australasia, where I was teaching animal communication workshops, I felt a strong pull to look at animal rescue websites, just as a magnet is drawn to its polar opposite, wishing to be together as one.

Every few days I was looking for 'the black dog' and waiting for a feeling of resonance that told me 'That's him.' None of the dogs I saw were making that connection, but Jo was thrilled I was engaging with the idea of a new dog in our lives.

Seven days after we got back to the UK, she said, 'I've got a dog I want to show you.'

I found myself looking at the 'Oldies' website, a website dedicated to finding homes for senior animals, and looking back at me was an old, tired-looking all-black dog with a huge amount of curly hair. I sat still and looked at him, but I didn't feel a stirring. There was no heart pang or leap in my stomach, no feeling of knowing without explanation. In my heart I knew he was not our dog.

But Jo was beyond desperate for a dog in her life. Something in me said to her, 'OK, give them a call. It will do no harm.'

It was this step that led to the next... and the step after that, each taking us a little further along the path to Morgan's predestined successor.

It is these moments of pulling and synchronicity that we need to pay attention to when we are searching for those we feel are destined to join us. Moreover, when we are bringing any animal companion into our life, it helps to listen to our intuitive feelings.

Once we've looked 'beyond cute' and addressed important practicalities – 'Is this animal a good fit for my family?' 'Do I have the lifestyle, time and finances to meet this animal's needs?' – it's really important to listen to that knowing that comes from the heart yet is so hard to explain.

The next day was Saturday and I was attending the first day of a weekend-long shamanic workshop. During that first day we were working with the energy of animals when I had the definite sense that the black dog was very close, but no logical explanation as to why.

When I arrived home Jo had a suppressed smile on her face that meant she was up to something – you know the kind of look a dog will give you when they're being a bit mischievous. After hearing about my day, she got to the cause of her restrained grin.

'I rang the rescue,' she told me, 'but they said that after many months of no interest the curly dog had four sets of people booked to visit him. They felt certain he would be adopted by one of them and said there was no point even going on a waiting list.'

She waited for dramatic effect; Pinter would have been proud of her pause.

'But then they said, "Have you seen Baxter?"'

'Baxter? Which one is he?' I quizzed. 'I don't remember another black dog.'

Straightaway Jo handed me her iPad. There was the image of a black dog.

Sitting down, I took all of a few seconds to look at him and acknowledge my rising excitement as a fluttering soared up from my solar plexus.

'*That's him! That's the black dog!*'

Very quickly my excitement turned to disappointment as I saw the word 'Rehomed'. The page said he'd arrived on 13 March and on 26 May he'd 'gone to his new home'.

'Well, he *had* been rehomed,' Jo explained with a smile, 'but when I rang them back the woman laughed and told me he was in his bed under the office counter beside her feet. She checked his records and he'd been rehomed months earlier but returned after just four days due to "a change in circumstances". She said we could view him tomorrow.'

Jo could hardly contain her excitement.

It dawned on me what had happened: no one had changed the availability status. The black dog had been 'on hold' at the home the entire time we'd been abroad. No one else had been able to adopt him because in the system he hadn't even existed. He'd already been earmarked... for us. He'd been waiting for the moment when we would finally discover him, the moment when I would be ready to welcome another dog into my heart.

Disappointed, I had to admit, 'I can't go tomorrow – I've got the course. Can you book us in to see him on Monday morning?'

Jo said she would and the following day at the workshop I tailored all my questions around the black dog 'on hold'.

In one shamanic journey I asked, 'Would a partnership with Baxter be for the highest good of my role in service?'

This was my most important question. I couldn't bring him into my life if he wasn't the dog Morgan had intended to take on his mantle. All professional animal communicators need a buddy to help them with their work. The animal isn't always a dog – cats, horses, rabbits and other species help some professional animal communicators.

The answer was immediate. In my mind's eye I saw a pure white horse rear in excitement and kick my left eye. It wasn't what I was expecting.

After the kick came a comment: 'The right one is OK.'

The horse was referring to my right eye. I wrote it down and the meaning of the message became apparent: 'The right one. Is OK.'

Baxter was the right black dog and it was OK, he was the right choice – full agreement.

I asked the horse, 'Why did you kick me?'

The response came, 'Because you'd only accept it hard and clear.'

It's true: I like things to be clear, especially when they are *so* important. I'm sure if I'd asked him again he would have given my left eye an even harder kick!

The Black Dog Encounter

Early on Monday we set off to meet Baxter. At first we were taken into a side room and a member of staff waxed lyrical about the rescue's positive points and dog training.

We asked about Baxter and were informed they'd collected him from a dog pound in South Wales, rescuing him from death row just before the seven-day execution. Jo and I looked at one another and grinned, because at that moment we'd received the final confirmation. Morgan had been rescued from South Wales and he had been on death row too. We'd wondered if there would be another sign in addition to my gut feeling that this black dog was the one. In our hearts we were now certain.

It was a useful sign, however, because when Baxter was finally brought out to us he didn't run up as if we were his long-lost friends or show us in any way that he knew we were coming for him. Instead he was distracted, anxious, keen to keep the one member of staff he felt safe with in his sight at all times.

We spent time together in a large enclosure and he ran up and down the wire fenceline trying to glimpse his sole human friend. When we took him on a short 'getting to know you' walk, he pulled and strained in his eagerness to move and sniff. He was kennel-stressed, under-exercised and suffering terrible separation anxiety. These factors also revealed themselves externally through appalling hair: his was dull and greasy with the most dandruff I'd ever seen on a dog. He was white speckled all over and he didn't smell too good either. He was also painfully thin – I could easily count seven visible ribs. Yet he was *our* black dog and in our eyes he *was* perfect.

We were told we could take him straightaway. We decided to take time out to be sure we were both fully committed, as it hadn't even crossed our minds we'd be taking him home that day. The process was feeling *very* fast.

We went to the local woods and discussed our feelings over tea and cake. Within hours Baxter was jumping effortlessly into the boot of our car and we were driving him home – to his forever home.

Over the next few days we discovered the full extent of his emotions. He was full of fear, needy and nervous, but this was nothing a large dose of love, good nutrition, plenty of off-lead exercise and clear guidance wouldn't rebalance. Principally, he needed to know he was safe.

His name didn't stay for long. As I grew to understand him, I felt 'Baxter' was too hard a name and didn't reflect his soft, sensitive nature. Jo quite liked it, but I just couldn't bring myself to say it. It took a few weeks before Jo and I came to rest on the answer – a name I knew would become *the one* the moment I laid eyes on it. It took Jo a little longer to come to the same conclusion. First, she tried Brodie, but it didn't trip off the tongue. His true name came into being a short time later: Bodhi. Bodhi means 'Enlightened one'. To me it just felt right.

Within 48 hours of our first encounter with the black dog, he had arrived in our home. But for the first week he howled, loudly, every night. We comforted him and day by day the howling diminished. Very soon all we needed to say was, 'You're safe, Bodhi, we're here,' and that would reassure him. With an improved diet, holistic supplements and homoeopathic treatment, his skin began to improve. With consistent love, exercise and clear guidance as to what was expected of him, he grew less anxious and more balanced. Very soon there was the regular sight of him sleeping upside down with all four paws up in the air, blissed out.

I'm not sure what lessons I am to learn from Bodhi. At the moment maybe it is enough for me to take the lead and learn new ways in order to help him rebalance. I do know that whenever I communicate with him he is lightning-fast in responding. There is no hesitation, so I know he has been here before. He is keen to be an active teacher in workshops, although he is not patient like Morgan: if you don't receive his message the first time, you may not get another chance. For many years I had no idea just how wise and powerful Morgan was, and maybe in time it will be this way with Bodhi too. At the moment it feels enough to know he has arrived, he is safe and the next leg of the journey has started. And there begins a whole new chapter...

But this book couldn't end without one last word from my teacher. So, here is Morgan with his message for you:

> *'Love – one word, one power. I have always felt that human beings lack love – love for others, love for themselves. It is true there is not enough love felt by beings, not enough love shared by beings. Why? I will leave that one with you.*
>
> *When I first met Pea, she was green. [Laughs.] No, literally, green in her outlook. Spiritually, she had so much to learn, so much to feel and experience to gain a greater understanding of her life and the life of others. Now I am proud to share what I feel: she is no longer green. Like you, Pea is learning a new way of being and existing in this world. Like you, she makes mistakes, doesn't always get it*

right and often does something stupid. The key is to try to learn, try to evolve, try to be more present in this world, both physically and on a spiritual level. It is not dualistic – it is all as one, joined at the hip, as you may say.

My role in life has always been to shine my love out into the world, whether through Pea, her work or in a more direct manner. It is a simple thing to do. Don't get me wrong – I am not asking for praise, as so many human animals do.

As Pea continues to learn that there is no separation in life and that physical life is merged with non-physical life, she will gain a greater understanding of this world and the universe, as will you all.

My purpose with this book has always been to open your eyes. To this world and the next. To the animals and the humans. To love and life and the meaninglessness of loss. Because there is no loss. I know you will struggle with this concept. But there is no loss, just a change in perspective. The physical form ends, this is true, but the spirit, the soul, the pure essence of that energy you call your "best friend" goes on and never dies, never ever. This is my truth. And I share it with you.'

Epilogue

Why a Black Dog?

‿✐

Initially, I was resistant to having a black animal in my life. Could it be that I held the archaic view that black animals were somehow lesser than those of other colours? One element of Bodhi's gift to me has been the dismantling of these ideas. How perfect that Morgan continued to teach me by sending me the embodiment of my prejudice.

In many cases people perceive black animals as dark, evil, devilish. But why should that be? Why is black considered the evil side of the polarity of good and evil? Is there such a thing as evil anyway?

A white dog triggered my wake-up call. I learned to connect with his inner light and also the light that is within me. Bodhi is the polar opposite to Morgan, the black to his white. And my learning continues with the black dog. The black is literally in front of my face. I am sure this is purposeful.

In Chinese philosophy the yin–yang symbol reveals how seemingly opposite elements are interconnected. They are independent but interrelate, forming a dynamic system in which the whole is greater than the parts. There are physical examples of this concept throughout nature, such as white and black, hot and cold, fire and water, high and low, life and death. In Taoist metaphysics, 'good' versus 'bad' distinctions are perceived moral judgements but not real, because yin–yang is an inseparable whole.

Heaven and Earth themselves are interlinked and part of a greater whole. So the energy of those in physical form and those in non-physical form are interlinked. My current belief is that there is the subtlest veil between this existence and the next, and it's only our mind that keeps us from accessing the world beyond – our heart knows the truth.

I also view the darkness, which Bodhi embodies, as a reminder to learn more about the shadow elements of myself as I continue to strive to bring each side of my energy, the yin and yang, back to wholeness and unity. What I believe now is that within the blackness is the most brilliant light: the two live together as One. Shadow cannot exist without Light.

Looking into our own shadow, our own void, is the same as exploring our subconscious nature. The shadow isn't evil, it is part of us, and black animals provide us with a visual reminder to open the door to that inner darkness. I believe one reason people are reluctant to fall in love with black animals is because they reflect that part of ourselves that we are afraid to touch. By discovering our shadow side and accepting the truth of who we are, we can raise our consciousness to an even greater level.

There is no such thing as an evil animal. It is just human projection that labels some evil, like black cats in some countries. Let us have reverence for black animals, because all species of animal, whatever their colour, are equal on the web of life and play an important part in evolution.

Now I am looking into the darkness and exploring its mystery. *Of course* a black dog – who else would be Morgan's successor?

Appendix

Empowering Animal Transition

A ll life is connected: the soul of an animal friend transitions out of the physical form, from one state of consciousness to another, but their love continues on.

Approaching a Beloved Animal's Death

How we approach a beloved animal's death can make the experience more difficult and painful or more beautiful and humbling. It is a great honour to be able to care for a dying animal.

Here are some suggestions to support an animal's soul journey and to support yourself as you adjust to the changes before you.

The Seven Gifts of Animal Soul Support

1. Keep it peaceful and quiet.
2. Play soft gentle music. Sometimes animals like to hear the sound of nature – the birds, waves or the wind. They often like gentle classical music.

3. Provide access to fresh air and a safe outside space.

4. Soften the lighting.

5. Make their environment as comfortable and uncluttered as possible.

6. Be mindful about visitors and prevent intrusions.

7. Honour their routine.

Seven Kind Ways to Support Yourself

1. Talk about your feelings with caring people who understand the depth of your relationship with your animal.

2. Spend quality time with your animal – if possible take some time off work to be with them before they transition.

3. Nourish yourself with healthy food, drink plenty of water and lessen the toxins you inflict on your body (alcohol, fast food, caffeine, etc.).

4. Be gentle with your body and lessen your expectations – work out gently or do regular stretching exercises, but don't push yourself hard. Walks are good.

5. Support yourself with a spiritual practice – meditate regularly.

6. Have some time away, preferably in nature, to ease your emotions, gain some perspective and rejuvenate your spirit.

7. Use lavender oil, Rescue Remedy, homoeopathy or crystals to support yourself, or any other method, like acupuncture, massage, etc., that helps you stay strong.

Give Permission to Let Go

One of the kindest things you can do for your animal is to give them permission to transition. Although animals are sentient beings who are equal to you, granting them permission to leave relieves them of any pressure they may feel to remain by your side. This concept is just as relevant for human beings. You might like to say the following:

> *'I love and honour you. I am ready for you to let go, in your own divine time, and give you my unreserved permission to transition. I understand our love will never end. May you be filled with Light to help you on your journey.'*

Honouring an Animal's Transition with a Ritual

Animals like a ritual that honours their soul. It is never too late to perform an honouring ritual for them, even after their transition.

There are no rules when it comes to celebrating an animal's life. You might like to:

◇ Write them a letter of gratitude.

◇ Read poetry or inspiring sayings of wisdom.

◇ Play music – chants, hymns, anything soothing.

◇ Light candles (a white one to represent their pure spirit) and invite the presence of those who love you both to support their transition.

◇ Create an ambience of calmness, love and respect.

◇ Gather together all the humans and animals they would like to be present. If they don't communicate their desire directly to you, trust your instincts.

◇ Create a special space with meaningful objects, e.g. a collar or toy.

◇ Look over photographs of your happy times together.

◇ Hang a photo of them up at home.

◇ Chant. *OM* is a good chant. It is a sacred sound that represents the most elemental sound of creation, or simply sing to them.

◇ Burn incense to guide their soul home.

Devotions

I would like to offer you a blessing and some prayers and poems you could read, either to yourself or out loud. These devotions are to help you align with the vibrations of courage and grace.

Blessing

<u>A Blessing for an Animal before Transition</u>
Dear friend, you are safe and with company.
I am by your side now and always with my love.
Release yourself from your tired body
and allow yourself to glide gracefully back home,
with my love and blessing,
until our souls embrace again.
You are loved.
I love you.

Prayers

<u>A Prayer for Guidance during Transition</u>
Beloved friends,
and all beings in this life and the next,
Please guide [animal's name] gently back home
to the place of love, peace and compassion,
to rest or play within Divine Grace,
full of love.
All is well.
And so it is.

A Euthanasia Prayer
Dear Guardian Angel of [animal's name],
I put my faith in the divine timing of this assistance.
Please guide [name] smoothly and
safely across to the other side.
I trust his/her spirit will be held with your grace and love
during the process of release from suffering physical form.
I trust you to assist this spirit release,
leading the way into the light.
I affirm my assistance is offered for
the highest good of [name].
My love is unconditional and I am willing to let go.
Thank you for your good grace.
All is well.

Poems

Honouring an Animal Who Has Transitioned
I honour your beautiful spirit,
your soul essence in my life.
I thank you for walking with me through part of my life,
for being so generous with your love and wisdom,
and for guiding me so gracefully through
your own life and transition.
You are a part of my heart and always will be.
I love you, I thank you and I honour you,
beloved friend.
Author unknown

The Feline Spirit

And God asked the feline spirit,
'Are you ready to come home?'
'Oh, yes, quite so,' replied the precious soul,
'and, as a cat, you know I am most able
to decide anything for myself.'

'Are you coming then?' asked God.
'Soon,' replied the whiskered angel.
'But I must come slowly,
for my human friends are troubled.
For you see, they need me, quite certainly.'
'But don't they understand,' asked God,
'that you'll never leave them?
That your souls are intertwined for all eternity?
That nothing is created or destroyed?
It just is... forever and ever and ever.'

'Eventually they will understand,'
replied the glorious cat.
'For I will whisper into their hearts
that I am always with them.
I just am... forever and ever and ever.'
Author unknown

I'm Still Here

Friend, please don't mourn for me,
I'm still here, though you don't see.
I'm right by your side each night and day
and within your heart I long to stay.

My body is gone but I'm always near.
I'm everything you feel, see or hear.
My spirit is free, but I'll never depart
as long as you keep me alive in your heart.

I'll never wander out of your sight –
I'm the brightest star on a summer night.
I'll never be beyond your reach –
I'm the warm moist sand when you're at the beach.

I'm the colourful leaves when fall comes around
and the pure white snow that blankets the ground.
I'm the beautiful flowers of which you're so fond,
The clear cool water in a quiet pond.

I'm the first bright blossom you'll see in the spring,
The first warm raindrop that April will bring.
I'm the first ray of light when the sun starts to shine,
and you'll see that the face in the moon is mine.

When you start thinking there's no one to love you,
you can talk to me through the Lord above you.
I'll whisper my answer through the leaves on the trees,
and you'll feel my presence in the soft summer breeze.

I'm the hot salty tears that flow when you weep
and the beautiful dreams that come while you sleep.
I'm the smile you see on a baby's face.
Just look for me, friend, I'm everyplace!
Author unknown

I Am Not There

Do not stand at my grave and weep,
I am not there; I do not sleep.
I am a thousand winds that blow,
I am the diamond glints on snow,
I am the sunlight on ripened grain,
I am the gentle autumn rain.
When you awaken in the morning's hush,
I am the swift uplifting rush
of quiet birds in circled flight.
I am the soft stars that shine at night.
Do not stand at my grave and cry.
I am not there; I did not die.

Mary Frye

Grieving

Grieving is a very personal experience. The way each of us grieves depends on many aspects, such as our coping ability, character, beliefs, life experiences and, of course, the nature of our loss.

Grief is a process. It involves our physical body, making us feel exhausted and in physical pain. It involves our emotional body as we go through a gamut of different emotions, some of which are familiar and some very new. It involves our spiritual body and over time we may have spiritual experiences, like being aware of the presence of our loved one who has passed over.

Grief comes from a deep desire for things to be how they were and involves coming to terms with how they are now. The loss of a beloved animal can be too intense to bear but eased when we're able to remember the truth: the living spirit of our loved one has separated from its physical form and gone to re-engage with Source.

At times the emotions can feel overwhelming and this is perfectly natural. When we grieve we are also celebrating the bond we had with our animal friend. So, we should not be afraid to cry.

Grief is an important part of our recovery. It's part of accepting they have passed over. Bottled-up grief can hurt us emotionally and physically, and it also prevents us from healing and engaging with life again. There are good days and bad days, and eventually we will notice the good days are outnumbering the bad ones.

Types of Grief

Psychologist, medical doctor and author of *Life After Life* Dr Raymond Moody divides grief into two main categories:

◊ *Acute* grief, which is when there is a sudden loss, such as a car accident that instantly kills an animal or a very sudden and extreme illness that leads to a quick death. These deaths are described as fast and unexpected.

◊ *Chronic* grief, which is when there is awareness that an animal is unwell and a gradual decline, such as I experienced with Morgan. It is in this gradual decline that, as the guardian, we experience *anticipatory grief*. It may be helpful to understand that when going through this pre-grief we are going through the same grief that is experienced after death. I have spoken to so many clients who feel they are 'falling apart' as their beloved animal is slowly approaching death. This is because they are experiencing anticipatory grief while trying to hold it together to care for their companion and provide them with a 'good death'.

◊ Additionally, there is also *disenfranchised* grief: grief that is not acknowledged by society. Much of society does not recognize that grief for an animal is as meaningful as grief for a human.

Please don't allow others views to define the depth of your love and the significance of your grief. Your emotions are real. Your grief is real, no lesser, nor unimportant. Grief is a universal emotion.

I hope to see a day when society acknowledges all grief as significant – regardless of species.

The Animal Thoughts Grieving Model: R-E-C-O-V-E-R

Rest: Grieving is exhausting, so allow yourself plenty of rest.

Exercise: Even just a little exercise will raise the level of your mood-enhancing endorphins.

Compassion: Be kind to yourself and don't have any expectations.

Open: Express your feelings and allow friends and family to support you.

Value: Create memories to celebrate your beloved animal.

Empower: Try and find new meaning and joy in your life.

Remember: Grief has no time limit and keeps to its own clock.

Affirmations

◇ 'I flow with my grieving process.'

◇ 'I learn to adjust to the changes within and outside myself.'

◇ 'I embrace my new life.'

Closure?

Closure is a very misused and unhelpful term. I feel it offers false hope because grief never really ends. It lessens and for moments it can be absent, as if it has evaporated altogether, but any other loss can trigger it all over again. Some people can feel as though they are experiencing all the losses they have ever had in their life all at once.

I don't feel closure is something we head for and once we've reached it we can 'move on'. A more balanced and realistic approach is to walk hand in hand with the process of grief and at some point you will discover a feeling of acceptance. This doesn't mark the end of grieving because the sadness tends to come in waves even when we feel acceptance.

Please be careful of any product or service claiming to offer closure. It's understandable to yearn for anything that will dull the agony or answer unresolved questions, but closure has been made into a commercial commodity, marketed for financial reward and consumed for a quick resolution. Grief doesn't work this way.

Getting Another Animal

'Should I get another animal right away?' is a question people often ask.

It is no coincidence that a lot of the behavioural concerns people have with new animals are due to bringing them into their lives as a mask for their sadness. The new animal may become stuck in the grief that is present, and while some animals are sympathetic and will try and take on our pain, others can find themselves, through no fault of their own, in a position of control and become unbalanced. It is best to wait until everyone feels they have mourned their loss and feels ready to welcome a unique, special being into their heart.

People also worry that they're replacing their deceased friend by getting another animal. My experience is that animals on the other side encourage their guardians to welcome another animal into their life and heart again. They understand that their guardians wish to experience an animal's love again.

In a sense you could view your wish to welcome a new animal into your life, home and family as a tribute to your other beloved friend. Share the love you have within you with another animal companion, because each relationship is unique, sacred and beautiful in its own way.

Additional Help

If you feel you need help with your grieving process, don't be afraid to contact an animal-friendly bereavement counsellor (*see Resources*).

Animals Grieve Too

Animals see death as a cycle of life and feel the same about grieving. It would be arrogant to think that only human beings have the capacity to grieve. I am sure you already knew, or at least know now that you have reached the end of this book, that other species on this planet experience emotions, including loss. Animals see this as a natural part of life, which they process in their own time. There are ways we can support them during this process.

Signs of Grief:

◇ Animals who are grieving may appear sad, depressed, disinterested in life or the daily routine.

◇ Their eating and sleeping habits may change.

◇ They may want to stick close to us all the time or be restless.

◇ Some will cry out in a distressed voice.

◇ Some may soil in the house or self-mutilate.

◇ They may also go looking for their friend.

Ways to Help a Grieving Animal:

◇ Create an opportunity for them to see and say goodbye to their friend – give them a chance to smell them.

◇ Respect the time they need to grieve.

◇ Maintain their routines as much as possible.

◇ Try and give them extra time and attention.

◇ Slowly try to lift their spirits by increasing their activity, playing games, going on longer walks (if appropriate) or taking them to places they really enjoy.

◇ Animals are generous souls and sometimes try to ease our pain by taking it on themselves; to be supportive, don't look to them to take your pain away.

Celebrating the Life of a Loved One

Any action that preserves the memory of your friend can be a healing experience. You might like to:

◇ Collect photos and put together a photo album or scrapbook.

◇ Plant something as a reminder of life and regeneration – a plant, tree or bush.

◇ Commission a painting or sculpture of your animal as a physical reminder.

◇ Scatter their ashes somewhere meaningful to you both: think of a location you can revisit.

◇ Keep their ashes in a meaningful place – perhaps create a sacred space.

◇ Bury your animal in your garden or a special animal cemetery and place a memorial plant or statue.

◇ Write your heart out – a poem, a story or a blog post of your memories together.

◇ Place photographs of your loved one around your home.

◇ Create a tribute online: a website, social media, etc.

◇ Keep a lock of their hair or fur.

◇ Hold on to their collar or favourite toy. Be careful not to throw all their toys out, as you may regret it later. If you need to, place them out of sight and come back to them later.

Resources

Animal Loss Support

UK

The Blue Cross Pet Bereavement Support Service
Helpline: 0800 096 6606
www.bluecross.org.uk/2083/pet-bereavement-support-service.
html

The Samaritans
The Samaritans provide confidential non-judgemental emotional
support, 24 hours a day, for people who are experiencing feelings
of distress or despair.
Helpline: 0845 790 9090
www.samaritans.org

Support Line
Support Line offers confidential emotional support to children,
young adults and adults by telephone, e-mail and post. They work

with callers to develop healthy, positive coping strategies, an inner feeling of strength and increased self-esteem to encourage healing, recovery and moving forward with life. They also keep details of counsellors, agencies and support groups throughout the UK.
Telephone: 01708 765200
www.supportline.org.uk

The Ralph Site
A not-for-profit website that provides support to pet owners around the loss of a beloved companion.
www.theralphsite.com

USA
The American Society for the Prevention of Cruelty to Animals (ASPCA)
www.aspca.org/pet-care/pet-loss

Petloss.com
www.petloss.com

Pet Loss Support Page
www.pet-loss.net

Australia
The Australian Directory of Human Animal Interaction Programs
http://www.humananimalinteraction.org.au/category/pet_loss_and_grief

Animal Welfare

I've been following a vegetarian diet for over 25 years through personal choice based on ethical reasons. When it comes to the domestic animals with whom I share my life, I feed my dog and cat an omnivorous and carnivorous diet respectively. I do this because animal-based foods are their personal choice.

As someone who identifies herself as a vegetarian, it is important to me that the food I feed my animals is ethically sourced. I look for organic, free-range, non-factory farmed and from a sustainable source. I also avoid foods that are labelled 'meat derivatives' and opt for those without artificial additives, preservatives, colourings and flavourings.

I believe the quality of the foods we choose has a direct effect on our animals' health as well as their behaviour. It also has a direct effect on how farm animals live.

For more information on welfare for farmed animals, understanding labels and making ethical choices, visit: Compassion in World Farming (UK), www.ciwf.org.uk.

Cremation Services

I feel I can only list Dignity individually as it is the only crematorium service I've experienced first hand:

Dignity (UK)
www.dignitypetcrem.co.uk

Here are some nationwide organizations who will be able to help you find a suitable local service:

UK

The Association of Private Pet Cemeteries and Crematoria (APPCC)
www.appcc.org.uk

USA

The International Association of Pet Cemeteries and Crematories (IAOPCC)
www.iaopc.com

Music

Here is a list of albums you may consider using to create a calm atmosphere or to soothe a grieving heart:

Ashana: *Beloved*

Bliss: *Flying Free*, *A Hundred Thousand Angels*

Deva Premal: *Into Light*

Heart of Compassion: *Songs for Grief, Loss and Recovery*

ABOUT THE AUTHOR

Pea Horsley is the founder of *Animal Thoughts*, an animal communication service.

Pea teaches workshops in animal communication, from beginner to advanced levels, as well as providing private mentoring sessions. She is available for animal communication consultations in person or over any distance via telephone, e-mail or Skype call. Her compassion, gentleness and integrity shine through every aspect of her work, both in the UK and abroad.

In addition, Pea is the author of the much-celebrated book *Heart to Heart: Incredible and heartwarming stories from the woman who talks with animals*, which is also published in Italian and Korean.

Pea tutors at the College of Psychic Studies in London and is a columnist for various spiritual and animal magazines.

'My personal passion is to empower others who wish to help animals and awaken to the teachings the animals wish to share.'
Pea Horsley

To contact Pea and for more information on her workshops and other services:

 pea@animalthoughts.com

 PeaHorsley

 AnimalTelepath

www.animalthoughts.com